Master Gregorius

The Marvels of Rome

Translated by
John Osborne

MEDIAEVAL SOURCES
IN TRANSLATION

31

MASTER GREGORIUS
THE MARVELS OF ROME

Translated with an
Introduction and Commentary

by

JOHN OSBORNE

PONTIFICAL INSTITUTE OF MEDIAEVAL STUDIES

Acknowledgment

This book has been published with the help of a grant from the Canadian Federation for the Humanities, using funds provided by the Social Sciences and Humanities Research Council of Canada.

CANADIAN CATALOGUING IN PUBLICATION DATA

Gregorius, Magister
  The marvels of Rome

(Mediaeval sources in translation, ISSN 0316-0874; 31)
Translation of: Narracio de mirabilibus urbis Romae.
Bibliography: p.
Includes index.
ISBN 0-88844-281-5

1. Rome (Italy)—Description—476-1420. 2. Rome (Italy)—Antiquities. I. Osborne, John Lawrence. II. Pontifical Institute of Mediaeval Studies. III. Title. IV. Series.

DG807.G73 1987   914.5′632044   C87-093466X

© 1987 by
Pontifical Institute of Mediaeval Studies
59 Queen's Park Crescent East
Toronto, Ontario, Canada M5S 2C4
Printed by Les Éditions Marquis Ltée, Montmagny, Canada

Distributed outside North America by
E.J. Brill, Leiden, The Netherlands
(Brill ISBN 90 04 08437 1)

Contents

Preface	vii
Introduction	1
Text	16
The Marvels of Rome	17
Commentary	37
Bibliography	101
Index	113

Preface

Since my first encounter with Magister Gregorius and his *Narracio de Mirabilibus Urbis Romae*, I have considered it to be one of the most intriguing literary products of the later Middle Ages—not because of the content of the work itself, however fascinating the descriptions of classical buildings and statues might be, but rather due to the unabashed antiquarian curiosity which is revealed by its author on page after page. This ardent desire to discover the truth, coupled with a healthy scepticism for popular accounts in an age better known for its unquestioning faith, distinguish Gregory and his *Narracio* from the wealth of topographical literature concerning Rome which has survived from the medieval period; and perhaps more than any of the objects which he describes, the real "marvel" is his attitude towards them. In some ways he seems little different from many modern art historians: scoffing at the tales told by local guides, measuring buildings, and returning three times to study a statue which appealed to him. These are actions which the reader can identify with, and therein lies Gregory's great appeal.

The *Narracio* is an extremely useful document for a variety of reasons. To begin with, it gives us some idea of the vast number of classical structures which still stood in the Middle Ages in Rome, as they must also have done elsewhere. The ancient Romans built to last, and the physical products of their civilisation endured far longer than the civilisation itself. Indeed most of their structures survived until someone made an effort to demolish them, usually with the aim of re-using the building materials. In Rome the great campaigns of demolition took place principally in the sixteenth and seventeenth centuries, and we often tend to forget how much of the ancient city was still available to the medieval viewer. Gregory reminds us. Secondly, he provides us with a great deal of information about the condition and placement of, in particular, statues, including some of the most famous bronzes to have survived into modern times. His is one of only two medieval references to the Spinario, for example. Furthermore, he gives us some idea of how these statues and buildings were viewed in the Middle Ages, both by the common people and by the best scholars at the papal court. It doesn't matter that their identifications were frequently, indeed usually, wrong.

Perhaps most important of all, the *Narracio* stands as an eloquent witness to a new attitude towards the physical inheritance from antiquity, no longer something simply to be gaped at or adapted to new uses, the bronze melted down, and the marble stripped away for the construction of churches. Rather, works of classical art are for the first time admired for their intrinsic beauty, and for the skill of the artists who produced them, instead of being feared as idols capable of bewitching men with evil spells. Gregory appears to be the first medieval writer to look at classical statuary with a critical eye, and the first to introduce a sense of aesthetics into the discussion, however underdeveloped that sense may be. He is perhaps the first connoisseur of ancient art, and for that reason alone deserves an important place in the history of the classical tradition.

Most of the initial research for this study was made possible by a travel grant from the University of Victoria. I would also like to record my gratitude to Avril Pedley, assistant librarian of St. Catharine's College, Cambridge, who permitted me to examine the only known manuscript copy of the *Narracio*; to the libraries of the Warburg Institute in London and the British School at Rome, where most of the research was undertaken; to the Master and Fellows of Corpus Christi College, Cambridge, in whose splendid company the work has been brought to fruition; and to the many individuals who have generously offered suggestions and advice, in particular to Ingo Herklotz, Dale Kinney, Richard Cocke, and Julian Gardner. Their help and encouragement has been invaluable.

Corpus Christi College
Cambridge
June 1985

Introduction

The *Narracio de Mirabilibus Urbis Romae*, written by an otherwise unknown *magister* Gregory, is a Latin text of approximately 4500 words in which the author describes the classical statues, buildings and other monuments which he has seen and examined in the city of Rome. At first known only through its partial incorporation in the *Polychronicon* of Ranulph Higden, monk at the Benedictine abbey of St. Werburgh, Chester, in the first half of the fourteenth century,[1] an independent and more complete copy of the work was discovered by M.R. James in the library of St. Catharine's College, Cambridge, and published by him in the 1917 issue of the *English Historical Review*.[2] Two years later, Gordon Rushforth published it again in the *Journal of Roman Studies*, incorporating a number of minor corrections to the Latin transcription and appending a lengthy introduction in which he suggested possible identifications for the marvels described by Gregory.[3] Rushforth's version of the *Narracio* was republished with additional notes by R. Valentini and G. Zucchetti in their compendium of medieval sources which deal with the topography of Rome,[4] and it also served as the basis for the only previous English translation, included by George Parks in his book

---

[1] Ranulph Higden, *Polychronicon*, ed. C. Babington (London 1865), 1: 206-238. See also John Taylor, *The 'Universal Chronicle' of Ranulph Higden* (Oxford 1966).

[2] M.R. James, "Magister Gregorius de Mirabilibus urbis Romae," *English Historical Review* 32 (1917), 531-554.

[3] G. Rushforth, "Magister Gregorius de Mirabilibus urbis Romae: a new description of Rome in the Twelfth Century," *Journal of Roman Studies* 9 (1919), 14-58.

[4] R. Valentini and G. Zucchetti, *Codice topografico della città di Roma* (Rome 1946), 3: 137-167. The authors acknowledge (p. 142) that they have reproduced Rushforth's text, "non essendo possibile, in questo momento, esaminare direttamente il codice."

The English Traveler to Italy.[5] An edition of the Latin text, incorporating further corrections, was published by R.B.C. Huygens in 1970.[6] Despite Rushforth's comment that his notes do not constitute a proper commentary, they are in fact the most detailed investigation of the text to have been undertaken thus far, and it is the aim of the present study to bring them up to date in the light of continued excavation and research over the past six decades.

The single extant copy of the *Narracio* is to be found in manuscript E IV 96 of the library of St. Catharine's College, Cambridge. This manuscript, which still retains intact its original binding and wooden covers, contains a number of medieval topographical and historical works in 204 folia.[7] The *Narracio* comes at the end of the volume, beginning after three blank leaves on folio 190r, and finishing abruptly at the end of the third line on folio 203r. The remainder of this leaf has been cut away, but there is no evidence to suggest that the text continued any further; the verso of the folio is blank, and there is nothing attributed to Gregory by Ranulph Higden which cannot be found in those chapters which have survived. Perhaps the author never completed his task.

The script of the Cambridge manuscript has been assigned to the late thirteenth century, and is written in what James describes as "a good clear English hand."[8] Its provenance is unknown, and it does not appear to have entered the St. Catharine's library until the first decade of the eighteenth century: it contains a bookplate of the year 1701, and James records a reference to it having been seen by a visitor to the college in 1710.[9] Because other portions of the manuscript were clearly written by the same hand, it seems most unlikely that this could be Gregory's autograph, and this view is strengthened by

---

[5] George B. Parks, *The English Traveler to Italy* (Rome 1954), 1: 254-268. A portion of this translation was included in C. Davis-Weyer, *Early Medieval Art, 300-1150. Sources and Documents* (Englewood Cliffs, N.J., 1971), pp. 158-162.

[6] Magister Gregorius, *Narracio de Mirabilibus Urbis Romae*, ed. R.B.C. Huygens (Leiden 1970).

[7] For a complete description of the contents see M.R. James, "Magister Gregorius," p. 532; or idem, *A Descriptive Catalogue of the Manuscripts in the Library of St. Catharine's College, Cambridge* (Cambridge 1925), pp. 10-12 (ms. no. 3).

[8] James, *A Descriptive Catalogue*, p. 10.

[9] *Ibid.*, p. 1.

the large number of orthographic errors, including many obvious misunderstandings of proper names. There are also errors of a type clearly attributable to transcription. For example, in the second sentence of chapter 23 the scribe's eye momentarily slipped from the correct line, and instead of writing "ubi archus iste triumphalis descriptus est" he has repeated the phrase "triumphales plures" from the previous sentence. Subsequently catching his error, he then crossed out "plures," although the final vowel of "triumphales" remains uncorrected. Variations between the text of this manuscript and that incorporated into Higden's *Polychronicon* suggest that the Chester chronicler did not use this particular copy.[10] Others must therefore have existed, but evidently none have survived.

M.R. James's division of the text into thirty-three chapters, based in part on rubrics contained in the Cambridge manuscript, has been followed in all subsequent publications. Gregory begins by describing the city as he himself first saw it, spread out before him as he descended the slope of Monte Mario. He then includes a list of the city's gates before embarking on his principal task, which is the enumeration of the many wonders to be found inside the walls. The arrangement of the subjects in the remaining chapters gives the impression that he began with some sort of structure for the *Narracio* in mind, but that this scheme rapidly fell by the wayside as one object or building led his mind to consider another. By the end of the work any semblance of a coherent structure has disappeared entirely.

Among the variety of objects and buildings which he encountered in Rome, he appears to have been particularly impressed by the statues cast in bronze (principally those which stood in the square adjoining the papal residence and cathedral of S. Giovanni in Laterano, which in a later age would form the nucleus of the Capitoline Museum), and he states that he will examine these bronze statues first. Following a brief account of a bull on the battlements of the Castel Sant' Angelo, we are then offered a lengthy discussion of the possible identification of Rome's most famous antique bronze, the equestrian monument of the second-century emperor Marcus Aurelius. This statue clearly

---

[10] For the relationship of the text to Higden see James, "Magister Gregorius," pp. 532-527, and Huygens, p. 7.

impressed our author greatly, and the two lengthy chapters devoted to it together comprise almost one-fifth of his entire work.

Next he turns his attention to the bronze head and hand, which he identifies as having come from Nero's Colossus (ch. 6). In this chapter we encounter for the first time Gregory's attempts to associate various marvels seen in Rome with those described in an anonymous medieval work entitled *De septem miraculis mundi*,[11] in this instance with the Colossus which straddled the entrance to the harbour of Rhodes. After a brief mention of the Spinario, or Thorn-Plucker, here curiously and uniquely identified as Priapus, he returns to the *De septem miraculis mundi* for accounts of other bronze statues which had formerly been in Rome (chs. 8, 9). However, there is no suggestion that they still stood in the city, or that Gregory had seen anything which resembled them, and presumably they are included simply to round out the discussion of works in the medium of bronze.

The following chapters mark the first principal departure from his intended structure. Having paused to include the bronzes described in the *De septem miraculis mundi*, he now introduces two other wonders from this text, and one of these, the bath of Apollonius of Tyana, he identifies with a hot sulphurous bath in Rome which he has paid an entrance fee to examine.

Chapter 12 opens with the announcement that the subject of marble statuary will now be considered, and both this chapter and the next are indeed devoted to that topic, describing a variety of marble pieces in the vicinity of the Quirinal hill. Then Gregory once again begins to get sidetracked. In the context of marbles on the Quirinal, his thoughts naturally pass to a group of horned images which he had seen on that hill in the "Palace of the Cornuti" (ch. 14), and subsequently to other large structures which have marble, although not

---

[11] The text of the *De septem miraculis mundi* is included in the *Patrologiae cursus completus, Series Latina*, ed. J. Migne, 90 (Paris 1862), 961-962. Later it would be frequently although falsely attributed to Bede, see Charles W. Jones, *Bedae Pseudepigrapha: Scientific Writings falsely attributed to Bede* (Ithaca, N.Y., 1939), pp. 89-90. The seven wonders are: the statues on the Capitol in Rome, the Pharos of Alexandria, the Colossus of Rhodes, the statue of Bellerophon at Smyrna, the theatre at Heraklea, the Bath of Apollonius of Tyana, and the temple of Diana at Ephesus. Gregory will include all of these but the last, and the extent of his direct quotation is examined by James, "Magister Gregorius," pp. 537-539. For further discussion see the commentary to chapter 6.

necessarily statues: for example the columns of the Baths of Diocletian (ch. 15), or the throne of Augustus on the Palatine (ch. 17). In the chapters which follow, the connecting relationships appear to depend more on geographic proximity than on subject matter, as thinking about one building in a certain region of the city leads him to recall another in the same area. Thus the account of the imperial palace is followed by a discussion of the nearby aqueduct (ch. 18), which in turn brings to mind the houses of Aquila and Fronto (ch. 19). Although there is no statement to this effect, we have clearly passed from marble statues to buildings, and Gregory next lists a number of "palaces," adding a remark about the difficulty he experiences in attempting to describe them adequately, before pausing to examine in greater detail the Pantheon (ch. 21). This then causes him to remember a nearby triumphal arch (ch. 22), which leads him to other triumphal arches and a triumphal column (chs. 23-26)

At the end of chapter 26 there is a clear break in the train of thought, and a new subject is announced: pyramids. Included in this group is the Egyptian obelisk which stood next to St. Peter's (ch. 29), here identified as containing the cremated remains of Julius Caesar, and a discussion of this tall monument with its animal supports again brings to mind a similar structure described in the *De septem miraculis mundi*, namely the Pharos at Alexandria (ch. 30). The mention of animal figures then leads him to a marble sow (ch. 31), and a bronze wolf (ch. 32), the latter evidently forgotten during the earlier enumeration of objects in this medium. While thinking of the wolf he remembers yet another bronze which stood near it, the "tablet prohibiting sin" (ch. 33), and at this point the *Narracio* breaks off rather abruptly. Given the inclusion of a lengthy prologue, one might have expected some sort of formal conclusion, or at the least a concluding statement, and thus the reader is left with the clear impression that the work as we have it is incomplete.

Although the *Narracio* is by no means the only medieval text to describe the city of Rome and its classical antiquities, it is unique in its complete preoccupation with the ancient world to the virtual exclusion of any interest in Christian Rome. St. Peter's and the cathedral of S. Giovanni in Laterano are mentioned only in passing, as geographic points of reference to locate the pyramid of Romulus and the papal collection of classical bronzes; and the only other church to be mentioned at all is S. Maria Rotonda, and then only because it was a re-used classical building, the Pantheon. The characters in Gregory's story are Scipio, Julius Caesar, Pompey, Brutus, Cassius, Augustus, Tiberius, Nero and Vespasian—and not, as we might have expected, Peter, Paul, Lawrence, Sylvester or even Constantine. In fact, apart from a brief reference to the martyr Hippolytus (ch. 16), the only Christian figure to intrude into this cast is the author's namesake, Pope Gregory I (AD 590-604), who appears three times in his role as the apparent villain of the piece: the man responsible for the destruction of many of the city's pagan monuments. It is interesting to note that this same role is also given to this pope by the twelfth-century English historian, John of Salisbury, who credits Pope Gregory with the destruction of the pagan library on the Palatine hill.[12] In John's account, this act is viewed with approval, but *magister* Gregory seems rather less than pleased with the papal actions, although he does not outrightly condemn them.

The author's curiosity to identify and explain the wonders of the city is indeed remarkable, and the text is enlivened by the inclusion of a number of personal glimpses. Gregory pays an entrance fee to bathe in the bath of Apollo, but is put off by the odour of the sulphur and only dips his hand in it in order to test the temperature; he paces off the width of the Pantheon, which he records as 266 feet; and he returns three times to examine a marble statue of Venus which has entranced him. Unlike most medieval visitors to the city, who came to venerate the relics of Peter and other early martyrs, the only remains which interest Gregory are those of Julius Caesar. His text is filled with quotations from or allusions to a variety of classical authors, but lacking a single line from the Bible or patristic literature, and in many respects his antiquarian concerns appear to foreshadow by some two or three centuries the better-known activities of this sort which characterize the Italian Renaissance.

It is primarily because of this attitude that the *Narracio* has drawn the interest of those historians who are concerned with the revival of interest in the ancient world which pervaded so many aspects of

---

[12] See T. Buddensieg, "Gregory the Great, the Destroyer of Pagan Idols. The History of a Medieval Legend Concerning the Decline of Ancient Art and Literature," *Journal of the Warburg and Courtauld Institutes* 28 (1965), 44-65; and the commentary to chapter 6.

scholarly activity in western Europe in the twelfth century. Ever since the concept of a twelfth-century "renaissance" was first developed half a century ago by Charles Haskins,[13] much has been made of the apparent concern for and interest in classical antiquities which can be documented in this period for the first time.[14] To be sure, there had always been an interest in putting classical objects and buildings to new uses in new contexts, from the widespread re-use of sarcophagi and Roman building materials, to the transformation of entire structures such as the Pantheon in Rome or the Parthenon in Athens, but this stemmed largely from the fact that fresh supplies of such commodities were less easily accessible in the Middle Ages (and when they were available, the quality of the workmanship was usually demonstrably inferior). However, what is new in the twelfth century is an apparent interest in antiquities for no reason other than that they were antiquities, the tangible manifestations of the ancient world in which much new interest was being taken. In this context it is not so surprising to encounter John of Salisbury's tale of Henry of Blois, bishop of Winchester, collecting classical statuary in Rome *circa* AD 1150 and shipping it back to England,[15] or to learn of the Roman Senate's decree of 27 March 1162 providing stiff penalties for anyone caught damaging the Column of Trajan.[16] In Rome itself, much of this new interest had conscious political overtones, being either an attempt to establish the ancient authority of the "Senatus Populusque Romanus," a concept newly revived in 1143, or to

---

[13] Charles H. Haskins, *The Renaissance of the Twelfth Century* (Cambridge, Mass., 1927).

[14] The literature is extensive, but see in particular James Ross, "A Study of Twelfth-Century Interest in the Antiquities of Rome," *Medieval and Historiographical Essays in Honor of James Westfall Thompson* (Chicago 1938), pp. 302-321; and Herbert Bloch, "The New Fascination with Ancient Rome," in *Renaissance and Renewal in the Twelfth Century*, ed. R. Benson and G. Constable (Oxford 1982), pp. 615-636.

[15] John of Salisbury, *Historia Pontificalis*, ed. R. Poole (Oxford 1927), p. 81: "Cum vero episcopus preter absolutionem se nichil optinere posse videret, accepta licentia rediens veteres statuas emit Rome, quas Wintoniam deferri fecit." See also Pietro Fedele, "Sul commercio delle antichità in Roma nel XII secolo," *Archivio della R. Società Romana di Storia Patria* 32 (1909), 465-470.

[16] See A. De Boüard, "Gli antichi marmi di Roma nel medio evo," *Archivio della R. Società Romana di Storia Patria* 34 (1911), 239-245, esp. 241 n.1.

strengthen the papal claim to have inherited the imperial mantle of the Caesars.[17] It is at this moment that the papacy enters what has recently been termed its "monarchic phase"[18] under the leadership of Innocent II (1130-1143), and it is no coincidence that this pontiff was addressed in court panegyrics as "Caesar," and that he was buried in what was believed to be the porphyry sarcophagus of the emperor Hadrian.[19]

But despite this well-documented revival of interest in the ancient world, there is a spirit in Gregory's *Narracio* which seems to go a step further than the other literary products of the period. Although Hildebert of Lavardin's poem "Par tibi, Roma," the first two lines of which are quoted by Gregory in his opening chapter, is typical of this new regard for antiquity in its nostalgic yearning for the glories of a lost golden age, before the city and its monuments had begun to fall into physical ruin, it is followed by a companion elegy in which Christian Rome responds to the author's lament, arguing that the Rome of Peter is nonetheless greater than the Rome of Caesar.[20] This seems to imply a rather different attitude from that of the *Narracio*, where the concern for antiquity is scholarly rather than emotional, and where there is never the slightest suggestion that contemporary or "Christian" Rome is of much interest.

The same distinction would appear to set Gregory apart from other contemporary or near-contemporary authors who describe the topography of the city, some of whom similarly include lengthy discussions of palaces, statues and other antiquities. The best known

---

[17] For this political context see Robert Benson, "Political 'Renovatio': Two Models from Roman Antiquity," in *Renaissance and Renewal in the Twelfth Century*, pp. 339-386, esp. pp. 340-359.

[18] Ernst Kitzinger, "The Arts as Aspects of a Renaissance: Rome and Italy," in *Renaissance and Renewal in the Twelfth Century*, p. 648.

[19] For a detailed examination of Innocent's deliberate choice of porphyry see Josef Deér, *The Dynastic Porphyry Tombs of the Norman Period in Sicily* (Cambridge, Mass., 1959), pp. 146-154. For the pope as "Caesar" see P. Schramm, *Kaiser, Könige und Päpste* (Stuttgart 1970), 4: 184 n.26.

[20] "Plus aquilis vexilla crucis, plus Caesare Petrus ..." The two poems are published in *The Oxford Book of Medieval Latin Verse*, ed. F. Raby (Oxford 1959), pp. 220-222. For Hildebert of Lavardin (ca.1056-1133) and his poetry see also F. Raby, *A History of Secular Latin Poetry in the Middle Ages*, 2nd ed. (Oxford 1957), 1: 317-329.

of these works are the *Mirabilia Urbis Romae*, compiled *circa* 1140 by a canon of St. Peter's, Benedict,[21] and the contemporary *Graphia Aureae Urbis Romae*, which includes much of the same material.[22] But despite their extensive enumerations of classical monuments, it is nonetheless a Christianized Rome which ultimately emerges. Thus the *Mirabilia* devotes a chapter to "haec ... loca quae inveniuntur in passionibus sanctorum," another to the early Christian cemeteries situated outside the walls, and a third to the persecution undertaken by the emperor Decius.[23] It attempts in general to construct a series of bridges between the pagan past and the Christian present, and thus it includes the tale of the emperor Augustus being shown a vision of the Madonna and Child by the Tiburtine sibyl,[24] and describes the replacement of pagan festivals and cults by appropriate Christian ones. It explains for example how the cult of St. Peter "in vinculi" came to replace the festival of Augustus on the kalends of August, and similarly how the Virgin Mary replaced Cybele as the "goddess" honoured at the Pantheon festival on the kalends of November, in each instance attempting to find a thematic parallel between the old and the new practices.[25] Christian Rome is seen as being constructed on the firm base of ancient Rome, which strengthens and enhances it; but one wonders whether Benedict could ever have been, as Gregory clearly was, interested in antiquities purely for their own sake. The *Mirabilia*'s viewpoint has been aptly described by Robert Brentano as "a sort of palimpsest with one civilization written over the other, or perhaps a tapestry with the two stitched together."[26] This statement is clearly not applicable to the *Narracio*, which in its

---

[21] For the text of the *Mirabilia* see R. Valentini and G. Zucchetti, *Codice Topografico* 3: 3-65. The identification of Benedict as the author was proposed by L. Duchesne, "L'auteur des 'Mirabilia'," *Mélanges d'archéologie et d'histoire* 24 (1904), 479-489.

[22] R. Valentini and G. Zucchetti, *Codice topografico* 3: 67-110. It has recently been linked with Montecassino, see H. Bloch, "Der Autor der 'Graphia aureae urbis Romae'," *Deutsches Archiv für Erforschung des Mittelalters* 40 (1984), 55-175.

[23] *Mirabilia*, chs. 8, 10 and 17.

[24] *Ibid.*, ch. 11.

[25] *Ibid.*, chs. 16 and 18.

[26] Robert Brentano, *Rome before Avignon* (London 1974), pp. 79-80. See also M. Adriani, "Paganesimo e cristianesimo nei 'Mirabilia Urbis Romae'," *Studi Romani* 8 (1960), 535-552.

extensive devotion to the vestiges of the ancient city makes no attempt to bridge the abyss between imperial Rome and papal Rome. It is also unique in that it offers an intensely personal view, and some of the descriptions suggest a measure of aesthetic appreciation of the sort which would develop and mature in humanist circles in the centuries to follow.

Given the obvious parallels to topographical works like the *Mirabilia*, and to the revival of interest in antiquities exhibited by the refounded Roman Senate and visitors to the city such as Henry of Blois, most scholars have sought to place Gregory's *Narracio* within the context of the twelfth century.[27] A fixed *terminus post quem* is established by his quotation of two lines from the poem "Par tibi, Roma" of Hildebert of Lavardin. One of the foremost classicizing authors of his age, Hildebert was born at Lavardin *circa* 1056, became bishop of Le Mans in 1096, archbishop of Tours in 1125, and died in 1133. His poems concerning Rome were composed following a visit to the city during the pontificate of Paschal II (1099-1118), and thus the *Narracio* could not be earlier than the first quarter of the twelfth century.[28] The *terminus ante quem* is established by Ranulph Higden's use of Gregory as a source for his *Polychronicon*, compiled in the third or fourth decade of the fourteenth century,[29] and by the St. Catharine's College manuscript itself, ascribed to the second half of the thirteenth century on the basis of its script. A composition date within the confines of the twelfth and thirteenth centuries is thus beyond dispute.

---

[27] First proposed by James, "Magister Gregorius," p. 543, and taken for granted by Rushforth who gives this dating in the title of his article. Most recently it has been supported by Herbert Bloch, "The New Fascination with Ancient Rome," p. 630, who places the *Narracio* "in the second half of the twelfth century (rather than early in the thirteenth)."

[28] For Hildebert *v. supra* note 20. The entire poem was reproduced *circa* 1125 by William of Malmesbury in his *Gesta regum anglorum* (4. 2), and the fact that Gregory refers to the poet as "quidam," and not by name, has prompted Rushforth (p. 16) to suggest that he knew Hildebert only at second hand, through an intermediary such as William. This argument is not entirely convincing, since William does name Hildebert, as too does Ranulph Higden when he includes the lines in his *Polychronicon*.

[29] For the *Polychronicon*, *v. supra* note 1. Huygens, pp. 43-44, provides a concordance of passages between the two texts.

There are two internal clues which may suggest that preference should be given to the latter half of this possible span, in other words to the thirteenth century rather than the twelfth. If Rushforth is correct in identifying the "horreum ... cardinalium," mentioned by Gregory in chapter 16, with the Tor de' Conti fortress established by the family of Pope Innocent III in the year 1203, then the range of possible dates is considerably narrowed.[30] Similarly, if Gregory's identification (ch. 29) of the astragals supporting "St. Peter's needle" as lions was based upon his having seen such figures supporting the Capitoline obelisk, and if Malmstrom is correct in believing that the latter was erected *circa* AD 1200,[31] then again the thirteenth century may be preferred to the twelfth. Such arguments are, however, exceedingly tenuous.

The reference in chapter 32 to a "winter palace" ("hiemale palatium") of the pope, which implies that in Gregory's time the papacy did not spend its summers at the Lateran, may also be helpful. Although the practice of moving the papal court out of the city during the unhealthy summer months can be traced back to the time of Gregory VII (1073-1085), it was principally a characteristic of the reigns of Innocent III (1198-1216) and Gregory IX (1227-1241), which would again suggest a date in the thirteenth century.[32] Regretfully there is little else in the text which may be deemed to have chronological significance, and thus one must conclude that there is no solid basis for narrowing further the range of possible composition dates.

It would of course be interesting to know something more about this curious antiquarian, but he himself provides little information concerning his identity. He tells us only that he was a *magister*. Until the early twelfth century this title was generally used to refer to the master in charge of a cathedral school, but by Gregory's time it was much more widely employed, indicating a man who had

---

[30] Rushforth, pp. 30-31, but see commentary to chapter 16.

[31] See discussion in commentary to chapter 29.

[32] This suggestion is proposed by Ingo Herklotz, "Der Campus Lateranensis im Mittelalter," *Römisches Jahrbuch für Kunstgeschichte* 22 (1985), 1-43, esp. 19 note 99, and 'Sepulcra' e 'Monumenta' del Medioevo (Rome 1985), p. 139. Pierre Toubert, *Les Structures du Latium Médiéval* (Rome 1973), pp. 1051-1054 discusses this annual migration, which he describes as a "véritable transhumance du personnel administratif."

received scholastic training.[33] There is no doubt that he was well educated, particularly in the fields of classical history and literature, since the *Narracio* contains five direct quotations from Lucan, three from Virgil, and one from Ovid, in addition to numerous indirect borrowings or probable allusions. The medieval sources which he uses—Isidore of Seville's *Etymologiae*, Hildebert of Lavardin, and the anonymous *De septem miraculis mundi*—are similarly secular in nature, and suggest wide-ranging academic interests.

Gregory was clearly a visitor to Rome and not a resident of the city, since he describes his first sight of its walls and towers (ch. 1) and also informs us that he was lodged at an inn (ch. 12); but his scorn for the fanciful tales circulating among the pilgrims who had come to venerate the city's shrines, and for their superstitious beliefs, suggests that he was not among their number. This view is strengthened by his apparent familiarity with members of the Roman *curia*. For example, we are told that his information on the working speed of stonemasons has come from the cardinals (ch. 15), as did his identification of the equestrian bronze (ch. 4). These are not the sort of contacts which average or casual visitors to the city would have had, and it seems likely, therefore, that he was engaged in some legal or diplomatic mission to the papal court. It was a business trip, although evidently one which allowed him a good deal of free time for sightseeing. Unfortunately the one word which might have solved the mystery of his origin, the place to which Gregory says he is returning (ch. 25), has dropped from the text as transmitted by the Cambridge manuscript (fol. 200r, line 16), nor is this section among those quoted by Higden. Rushforth suggests that the copyist did not recognize the name, and thus omitted it,[34] but there is nothing to indicate that this act was deliberate.

Most scholars have taken it for granted that Gregory was English, and indeed there are two major pieces of circumstantial evidence which point strongly in this direction: the single extant manuscript is in England and appears to be written in an English hand, and the

---

[33] See discussion by R.W. Southern, "The Schools of Paris and the School of Chartres," in *Renaissance and Renewal in the Twelfth Century*, pp. 113-137, esp. 134-135. The author notes that by 1200 almost half of the members of English cathedral chapters were *magistri*.

[34] Rushforth, p. 18.

only subsequent medieval author to use the *Narracio* was similarly English (namely, Ranulph Higden). His nationality thus seems reasonably secure, and a work such as this would not have been at all out of place in the context of the intellectual life of late twelfth or thirteenth-century England, which had a demonstrated fascination for the wonders of foreign lands.[35]

Some writers have attempted to be even more specific. Max Manitius, who wishes to locate Gregory in Canterbury, raises the possibility that the "dominus Thomas" referred to in the prologue might be that city's famous archbishop, Thomas à Becket (1162-1170).[36] This is an intriguing suggestion, and it certainly merits consideration. Thomas à Becket did not visit Rome during his tenancy of the see of Canterbury, although he had been there some twenty years earlier, but it should not be necessarily assumed that the Thomas who was encouraging Gregory to put pen to paper was a participant in the Roman journey. There is no indication as to how much time has elapsed between the visit to the city and the time of writing: it might have been weeks, months or many years. Similarly, although Gregory does imply (ch. 25) that the *Narracio* is not being composed at his place of residence, where he would have had greater access to books on Roman history, one should be wary of jumping to the conclusion that it is being written during the course of the homeward journey from Rome. This may indeed have been the case, but there are also other possibilities. For example, if he was in the employ of the archbishop of Canterbury, he may well have been living with his master in exile in France, whence Thomas did send delegations to Rome to present his case to Pope Alexander III. However, there is no known "magister Gregorius" who can be connected with him.

---

[35] R.W. Southern, "The Place of England in the Twelfth-Century Renaissance," *History* 45 (1960), 201-216, without referring specifically to Gregory's *Narracio*, views this type of literature as a particularly English contribution to late medieval culture in Europe. A further English link is provided by similarities to Alexander Neckam's *De naturis rerum* (see commentary to chapter 8). For the wealth of classical literature available to scholars in England in the late Middle Ages see R.A.B. Mynors, "The Latin Classics Known to Boston of Bury," in *Fritz Saxl (1890-1948). A Volume of Memorial Essays from his Friends in England*, ed. D. J. Gordon (Edinburgh 1957), pp. 199-217.

[36] See M. Manitius, *Geschichte der lateinischen Litteratur des Mittelalters* (Munich 1931), 3: 248.

In the light of those clues, previously mentioned, which may suggest a thirteenth rather than a twelfth-century date, there is a second and indeed more likely possibility. Josiah Russell has identified the author of the *Narracio* with an employee of Otto of Tonengo, a papal legate to England. Otto was in England for almost four years, from the spring of 1237 until January 1241, and the *Calendar of Patent Rolls* records that on 8 May 1238 the English king, Henry III, granted to the legate's chancellor, a certain "magister Gregorius," an annual pension of seventeen marks from the income of the bishopric of Norwich, to be paid as long as the see of Norwich should remain vacant. Revenues from vacant sees were paid to the royal treasury, and the pension was to be drawn from these funds. The matter is made particularly interesting by the information that this Gregory had previously received such a pension from the bishop of Norwich, recently deceased. The bishop's name was Thomas.[37] This coincidence of a "magister Gregorius" with a "dominus Thomas" does seem rather striking, particularly as the name Gregory appears only rarely in English documents of this period. Russell does raise one possible objection to his own suggestion: Thomas de Blandeville, bishop of Norwich, died in August of 1236, and Otto of Tonengo arrived in England only in 1237. However, the objection is easily countered. To begin with, this was not Otto's first journey across the English Channel: in 1225 he had been sent as papal nuncio to England by Pope Honorius III, and he may have encountered Gregory then, or in some other place subsequently. However, given the unusual nature of the post of *cancellarius* to a papal legate, a title with few known parallels in the first half of the thirteenth century, it seems more likely that the position was created *ad hoc* by Otto, when it became apparent that his stay in England would be a lengthy one. In such an event he would probably have employed someone from among suitable applicants available at hand, and the elevation in status stemming from such an appointment may well have afforded Gregory the opportunity to successfully petition the king for a continuation

---

[37] See Josiah C. Russell, *Dictionary of Writers of Thirteenth Century England* (London 1936), pp. 40-41, and Agostino Paravicini Bagliani, *Cardinali di Curia e 'Familiae' cardinalizie dal 1227 al 1254* (Padua 1972), p. 94. Bagliani appears to be the only subsequent scholar to have noted Russell's suggestion.

of his Norwich pension, the payment of which had been interrupted by the death of his previous patron. If Otto's chancellor was indeed our *magister* Gregory, then the date of the *Narracio*'s composition could be limited to the decade between 1226 and 1236, when Thomas was bishop of Norwich.[38]

In the absence of any secure documentation, however, the questions of the precise date of the *Narracio* and the identity of its author must in the end remain open. But this does nothing to detract from the value of the text and its importance for historians of the classical tradition.

---

[38] Thomas de Blandeville was elected bishop of Norwich in October 1226, consecrated on 20 December of the same year, and died on 16 August 1236; see Barbara Dodwell, *The Charters of Norwich Cathedral Priory* (London 1974), p. xlvi. His episcopal charters, published by Dodwell (pp. 103-113) were frequently witnessed by *magistri*, principally his chief official, *magister* Alan of Beccles, but Gregory's name does not appear among their number.

Text

The translation of Gregory's *Narracio* which follows is based on Huygens's 1970 edition of the Latin text, and while the meaning of some passages has on occasion been rendered rather freely, wherever possible an attempt has been made to retain the language and phrasing of the original. The brief notes at the end of the translation are limited primarily to the identification of quotations. Discussion of the content is left for the commentary.

The Marvels of Rome

Prologue

Here begins Master Gregory's prologue concerning the wonders which once were or still are in Rome, of which the traces or the memory remain alive to this day.

At the special request of my comrades, specifically Master Martin, Lord Thomas, and several others whom I greatly respect, I have been constrained to set down on paper those things which I have seen in Rome that are most worthy of admiration. I fear however that my poorly-composed report may disturb your sacred study and interrupt the delights of holy scripture, and I blush to offend ears accustomed to the lectures of the foremost scholars with my unpolished prose. After all, who wouldn't think twice about inviting to a plain and frugal repast guests who are accustomed to delicacies? That explains why my lazy hand has had to be prodded to take up the promised task, for often, just as I was about to pick up my pen, my mind would shrink from the subject when I considered the poverty of my disordered discourse. However, the wishes of my colleagues have finally overcome my bashfulness. In order not to delay the promised truth I have taken up the pen in my awkward clumsy hand, and I have set forth the work, as best I can, in the following manner.

The prologue ends.

Here begins the account of the wonders of the city of Rome, which have been fashioned either by magic craft or by human labour.

1

I strongly recommend the wonderful panorama of the whole city. There is so great a forest of towers, and so many palatial buildings, that no one has counted them. When I saw it for the first time, at a distance from the slope of the hill, my mind was struck by those words which Julius Caesar uttered after he had conquered the Gauls, flown across the Alps, and was greatly "admiring ... the walls of Rome:

> Home of the gods, have men abandoned you without a fight? What city will they then defend? Heaven be thanked ..."[1]

and so on. And a little later:

> "The city which could have held the throng of assembled humanity was abandoned by a cowardly hand,"[2]

and invoking the name of Rome, he called it

> "the image of the highest divinity."[3]

After I had spent some time admiring this stunningly picturesque sight, I thanked God, mighty throughout the entire world, who had here rendered the works of man wondrously and indescribably beautiful. For although all of Rome lies in ruins, nothing intact can be compared to this. And thus someone has said:

> "Rome, although you are almost a total ruin, you have no equal; Shattered you can teach us, whole how greatly you would speak!"[4]

I believe this ruin teaches us clearly that all temporal things will

---

[1] Marcus Annaeus Lucanus, *De bello civili* 3. 91-93.
[2] *Ibid.*, 1. 511-514.
[3] *Ibid.*, 1. 199-200.
[4] The opening lines of a poem by Hildebert of Lavardin (see Introduction), and Gregory's only direct quotation from a contemporary medieval source. For the complete poem see *Hildeberti Cenomannensis episcopi carmina minora*, ed. A. Brian Scott (Leipzig 1969), pp. 22-24. It should be noted that while the first line is quoted correctly, the second line ("fracta docere potes, integra quanta fores") is rather different from Hildebert's "quam magni fueris integra fracta doces," although clearly based on it.

soon pass away, especially as Rome, the epitome of earthly glory, languishes and declines so much every day.

2

The city has fourteen gates, named as follows: Porta Aurea, Porta Latina, Porta Sacra, Porta Salaria, Porta Marcia, Porta Livia, Porta Collatina, Porta Flaminia, Porta Numantia, Porta Appia, Porta Tiburtina, Porta Aquileia (which is now called the Gate of St. Lawrence), and the Porta Asinaria.

3

Let me begin with an account of the city's bronze statues. Concerning the first bronze statue:

The first bronze statue is a bull, like the one which, according to legend, Jupiter used to fool Europa. This statue projects from the fortifications of the Castle of Crescentius, and is so skillfully made that it appears to its viewers likely to bellow and move.

4

Concerning the second statue:

There is another bronze statue in front of the papal palace: an immense horse, with a rider whom the pilgrims call Theodoric, although the Roman people say he is Constantine, and the cardinals and clerks of the Roman curia call him Marcus or Quintus Quirinus. In ages past this memorial, made with extraordinary skill, stood on four bronze columns in front of the altar of Jupiter on the Capitoline, but blessed Gregory took down the horse and rider, and placed the four columns in the church of St. John Lateran. The horse and rider were set up outside the papal palace by the Roman people. The horse, the rider, and the columns were lavishly gilded, but in many places the gold has fallen victim to Roman avarice, and time has also taken its toll. The rider raises his right hand, as if to address the people or to give orders; his left hand holds a rein, which turns the horse's head aside to the right, as if he were about to ride away in another direction. A little bird, which they call a cuckoo, sits between the ears of the horse, and under the hoofs there is a sort of dwarf, who is being trodden upon. He makes a wonderful image of the agonies of death.

Just as this admirable work has been assigned different names, so too have a variety of reasons been proposed for its manufacture. I shall give a wide berth to the worthless stories of the pilgrims and the Romans in this regard, and shall record what I've been told by the elders, the cardinals, and the men of greatest learning. Those who call him Marcus give this account of its origin. There was a certain king of the Miseni, a dwarf, who was more skillful than any other man in the perverse arts of magic. After he had subjugated the neighbouring kings, he attacked the Romans, whom he easily defeated in several encounters. For his magic so blunted his enemy's strength and the keenness of their weapons that they completely lost the will to fight, and their weapons the power to inflict wounds. Because he defeated the Romans easily in every engagement, they were reluctant to leave their fortifications, and eventually found themselves surrounded by a tight blockade. Penned up in this way, they were unable to obtain any reinforcements.

Every day before dawn this magician would come out of his camp alone, and while the loud cry of a bird could be heard coming from the camp, he would practise his magic arts alone in a field. By certain secret words and powerful spells he made it impossible for the Romans to muster their strength and defeat him.

When the Romans became aware of this, and when they realized that he made a habit of leaving his camp in this manner, they approached a certain soldier named Marcus, a man brimming with energy, and promised him the highest honours if he would brave the danger and lift the siege of the city. They offered him its lordship if he could save it, and promised him an eternal memorial. He agreed, and that night they made an opening through the wall and its outer earthwork, so that this soldier and his horse could pass through to the spot where the king came out. Then they explained their plan. Marcus was to go out by night, and when he discovered that the king of the Miseni had left his camp, he was not to attack him with his weapons, since these had no power to hurt the king, but to seize him and carry him back inside the walls. Marcus gave his complete assent, and in the middle of the night he passed through the wall. Vigilantly he waited for dawn, and as usual the cuckoo began to sing, a sign of light in the eastern sky. Thus alerted, he mounted his horse, caught sight of the king, who was just beginning to perform his magic rites, and making a great charge, he siezed him. Captured in a manner he had not foreseen, the magician was then carried back inside the wall, and fearing that any delay might allow their captive to free himself by his magic craft, Marcus trampled him to death beneath the hoofs of his horse as everyone looked on; for the king could not be harmed by weapons. Then they opened the gates and fell upon the army, which, demoralized by the demise of its king, had begun to take flight; and in that fight a great many were captured or killed. Never have the spoils of battle so greatly enriched the Roman treasury, and because of the benefits gained from Marcus's participation, a memorial was put up in his honour as agreed. The horse, which had contributed its speed, and the bird, who had heralded the dawn, were also included; and the trampled dwarf was set beneath the horse's feet, where he had fallen.

5

Another explanation of this statue:

Those who call him Quintus Quirinus tell this story. In the days when Quintus Quirinus ruled the republic, a great chasm opened in the ground at the Palace of Sallust, spewing forth sulphurous fire and foul air. This caused a terrible plague which killed a great many Romans. When the daily death toll from this pestilence began to mount, the citizens consulted Phoebus and discovered that it would only abate if some Roman were to set the well-being of the populace ahead of personal considerations and willingly throw himself into the chasm. Accordingly a certain Roman citizen, of good family but getting on in years and leading an inactive life which brought no benefit either to himself or to his city, was implored to sacrifice himself for the common good, in return for which his family would be showered with wealth and raised to the ranks of the ruling class. He refused categorically, replying that the recognition of posterity was of little use to him if he had to enter the underworld alive.

When no one could be found in the whole city who would consent to perform this act of self-sacrifice, Quintus Quirinus addressed an assembly of the entire population: "In crucial wartime emergencies I have often risked death for the republic. Now, since no one can be found who considers the public welfare more important than his own personal safety, I the prince, lord of the world and this city, for the civic good, am prepared to pass alive through the portals of Hell; and those rewards which have been offered to cowards I want firmly preserved for my wife, my children, and all my descendants." Undaunted and in high spirits, as if on his way to a party, he mounted his horse, and in full view of everyone hurled himself at great speed into the opening. Immediately a cuckoo flew out, the chasm closed its jaws, and the plague departed.

Thus freed from this great curse, the Romans erected an eternal memorial in his honour, because of this supreme act of service. To this they added the horse, because Quintus had made his sacrifice while mounted on it. Between the ears of the horse they placed the bird which had flown out of the chasm, and beneath the horse's hoofs they put the dwarf who lay with his wife.

6

Concerning the third bronze statue:

The third statue is that of the Colossus, which some think to be a statue of the sun, while others call it the image of Rome. What is particularly astounding about this piece is how so great a mass could have been cast, how it was raised, and how it could stand. For its height, as I have discovered it written, was 126 feet. This enormous monument stood on the island of Herodius,[5] at the Colosseum, fifteen feet higher than the loftiest points in the city. It held a sphere in its right hand, and a sword in its left, the sphere representing the world, and the sword military prowess. The Romans entrusted the sword

---

[5] It is not certain what Gregory meant by the phrase "in insula Herodii." His source, the *De septem miraculis mundi*, refers of course to the island of Rhodes, but in transferring the statue to Rome he may well have been taking "insula" in its other sense, as a large apartment block. See James, "Magister Gregorius," p. 539.

to the left hand and the sphere to the right because it is more virtuous to rule than to conquer. As a philosopher has said: "It's easier to get to the top of the ladder than it is to stay there."[6]

The sphere was given to the side of strength and the sword to the side of weakness for no other reason than this: that it's less praiseworthy to conquer the world than it is to keep it conquered.

This bronze image was completely gilded with imperial gold and it shone in the darkness. The strangest thing of all about it was that it turned continuously in a motion equal to that of the sun, which it therefore always faced, and because of this many believed that it was the image of the sun. While Rome flourished, every visitor to the city worshipped it on bended knee, offering honour to Rome by worshipping its image. But after all the statues in Rome were pulled down and broken, blessed Gregory destroyed it in the following manner. Because such a great mass could not be toppled even by enormous effort and force, he commanded that a large fire should be lit under the statue, and this reduced the gigantic figure to its former formless state. The head, and the right hand holding the sphere, did however survive the fire, and these make a wonderful sight for onlookers, elevated on two marble columns in front of the papal palace. Although of horrific size, one can nonetheless admire in them the great skill of their maker, and indeed nothing of the perfect beauty of the human head or hand is lacking in any part. It's quite amazing how the fluid craftsmanship can simulate soft hairs in solid bronze, and if you look at it intently, transfixed by its splendour, it gives the appearance of being about to move and speak. They say that no other statue was ever made in the city with such care or expense.

7

Concerning the ridiculous statue of Priapus:

There is another bronze statue, a rather laughable one, which they call Priapus. He looks as though he's in severe pain, with his head bent down as if to remove from his foot a thorn that he had stepped on. If you lean forward and look up to see what he's doing, you discover genitals of extraordinary size.

---

[6] More literally: "O gods, you are ready to give men the best things, but less prompt to let us keep them." Lucan, *De bello civili* 1. 510-511.

8

Concerning a great many statues:

Among all the strange works which were once in Rome, the multitude of statues known as the "Salvation of the Citizens" is to be much admired. By magic art statues were dedicated to all those peoples who were subject to Roman rule, and indeed there was no race or region under Roman authority which did not have its statue in this particular hall. A large portion of its walls still stand, and the vaults seem stark and inaccessible.

In this hall these statues stood in a row, each one having written on its breast the name of the race which it represented, and each wearing around its neck a bell made of silver, because silver is more resonant than other metals. And there were priests who watched over them, ever vigilant both by day and by night. If any nation dared to rise in rebellion against Roman rule, its statue would immediately move, causing the bell to ring, and at once a priest would write down its name and convey this to the government. Above this hall of statues there was a bronze soldier on horseback who would move in conjunction with the statue, aiming his lance at the race whose image had stirred. Warned in this unequivocal manner, without delay the Romans would despatch an army to suppress that nation's rebellion, and they would often forestall their enemies before they could prepare their weapons and supplies, thus subjugating them easily and without bloodshed.

They say moreover that in the same hall there was an inextinguishable fire. When the artificer of this wonderful work was asked how long it would burn, he replied that it would last until a virgin gave birth. I'm told that the hall and the soldier collapsed in a great heap on the night that Christ was born of the Virgin, and that its magic artificial fire was justly extinguished when the true eternal light made its appearance. We can also believe that the evil enemy lost its ability to deceive mankind when God took human form.

9

Concerning the iron statue of Bellerophon:

There was in Rome an incredible wonder, an iron statue of Bellerophon and his horse, positioned in mid air, neither suspended from above by any chain nor supported by any post beneath. You see, the vault had an arc of magnetic stones on each side, which attracted the statue proportionately from different directions, and thus it remained balanced. Its weight was thought to be about 15,000 pounds of iron.

10

Concerning the bath of Apollo Bianeus:

Also much to be admired is the bath of Apollo Bianeus, which still exists in Rome. This bath was made with great skill in a bronze vat from a certain formula of sulphur, black salt and tartar. When it had been prepared, Apollo Bianeus lit it with one consecrated candle, and it was thereafter kept hot by a continuous fire. I saw this bath myself and I dipped my hand into it, but although I had paid the fee I declined to bathe because of the foul stench of the sulphur.

11

Concerning the theatre in Heraklea:

Among these marvels I shan't hesitate to record the wonderful theatre in the marble mountain at Heraklea. It was fashioned in such a way that all the rooms in the structure, all the seats in the amphitheatre, and all the exit ramps and caverns were carved from a single solid stone. This whole work is supported by six crabs, carved from the mountain itself. Here no one can speak secretly, either to himself or another, without everyone in the amphitheatre hearing.

Thus far I have discussed those things which are most deserving of admiration.

12

Now I shall turn my attention to the marble statues, almost all of which were destroyed or toppled by blessed Gregory. I shall begin with one in particular because of its exceptional beauty.

This statue, dedicated by the Romans to Venus, stems from the myth which relates that in a rash competition she, along with Juno and Pallas, displayed herself naked to Paris. Contemplating her, the thoughtless judge said: "In our judgment Venus conquers both."[7]

This image is made from Parian marble with such wonderful and intricate skill, that she seems more like a living creature than a statue; indeed she seems to blush in her nakedness, a reddish tinge colouring her face, and it appears to those who take a close look that blood flows in her snowy complexion. Because of this wonderful image, and perhaps some magic spell that I'm unaware of, I was drawn back three times to look at it despite the fact that it was two stades distant from my inn.

Close by there are two marble horses of incredible size and skillful composition. It is said that they represent the first mathematicians, to whom horses were assigned because of the quickness of their intellects.

13

Next to these, under two arches, lie two marble statues of old men, each stretched out some forty feet in length. They call one Solomon, the other Father Liber; Bacchus holds a vine branch in his hand, and Solomon a sceptre.

---

[7] Clearly alluding to Publius Ovidius Naso, *Ars amatoria* 1. 248: "cum dixit Veneri 'vincis utramque, Venus'."

14

Concerning the Palace of the Cornuti:

Near these is the Palace of the Cornuti, a large and towering structure in which there are many statues, all with horns. One among them, considerably larger than the others, is called Jupiter of the sands; but more reliable witnesses say that the Cornuti were the family who constructed that palace. Since they were both proud citizens and fierce opponents, they were important and well-known in the city, and were called "Cornuti" by their fellow citizens.

15

Concerning the Palace of Diocletian:

In this account of the city's monuments[8] I mustn't forget to mention the Palace of Diocletian, although words are not adequate to describe its vast size and its most skillful and admirable construction. It's so large in fact that I couldn't get an accurate impression of the whole structure despite spending the best part of a day there. I discovered columns so large that no one can throw a pebble as high as their capitals, and the cardinals say that a hundred men could scarcely cut, polish and finish one of these in the space of a year. I shan't say any more about it, since if I tell the truth you won't believe me.

16

Concerning the Temple of Pallas:

The Temple of Pallas was once a remarkable structure. Although demolished by the exertions of the Christians and crumbling with age, it hasn't been entirely destroyed, and the part which remains is used by the cardinals as a storehouse. There is a great heap of broken statues there, but also one of Pallas bearing arms which still projects

---

[8] It has been suggested that the phrase "urbis opus" is borrowed from Publius Vergilius Maro, *Aeneid* 5. 119 (cf. Rushforth, p. 16).

above the highest vault. Although disfigured by the loss of her head, spectators consider her a wonderful sight.

This statue was greatly venerated by the ancient Romans. Christians were led to it, and those who didn't worship Pallas on bended knee were executed by various means. Hippolytus and his family were brought to this image or idol, and when he paid it no obeisance he suffered martyrdom, torn apart by horses.

17

I can't leave out the palace of the divine Augustus, for the excellence of this vast dwelling equals that of its founder. Built entirely of marble, it has supplied a great deal of precious material for the construction of Rome's churches; but as so little of it remains, I shall say very little about it. A small portion of the throne does however survive, and on it I found this inscription: "the house of the divine and most merciful Augustus." For although he ruled the city and the entire world, he always avoided the title "Lord."

18

Beside the palace there is a brick wall which comes down from the mountains. Its enormous arches carry an aqueduct, through which a torrent flows from mountain springs, reaching the city in the space of a day. Split up by copper pipes, it once serviced all the palaces; for the river Tiber, which flows through the city, while fit for horses, is considered unsafe and harmful for men. Because of this the ancient Romans brought fresh water by artificial courses from the four corners of the city, and as long as the Republic flourished, anyone wanting water could take it. Adjoining the aqueduct, which comes down past the Porta Asinaria, is the bath of Apollo Bianeus. Once set alight by a consecrated candle, this bath produced continual heat, as I have related.

19

Near this bath are the houses of Aquila and Fronto. But who really cares whether I describe at length all the palaces in the city of Rome, since I'm sure that no one could ever see them all? Therefore I shall skip the enormous structure which was the palace of Tiberius, and leave aside the palace of Nero, the wonderful building of the divine Nerva, and the palace of Octavian. I shall not even speak of the seven thrones, skillfully constructed at great height, about which, they say, Ovid wrote:

> "The palace of the Sun towered on lofty columns, made bright by gleaming gold and flame-like bronze."[9]

20

Concerning the palace of the sixty emperors:

Who could describe the palace of the sixty emperors? Although much of it has crumbled, they still say that all the Romans of this day and age couldn't destroy what's left.

21

Concerning the Pantheon:

I shall only briefly mention the Pantheon, once the idol house of all the gods, or rather of all the demons. This building is now a church dedicated in honour of all the saints, although it is generally called S. Maria Rotonda. It has a spacious portico, supported by many lofty columns, and in front of it there remain to this day a basin and other wonderful porphyry vessels, as well as lions and other statues made of the same material. I measured the width of the structure and found it to be 266 feet. The roof was once completely gilded, but excessive avarice and the "accursed greed for gold"[10] have caused the Roman people to scrape away the gilt and disfigure

---

[9] Publius Ovidius Naso, *Metamorphoses* 2. 1-2.
[10] Virgil, *Aeneid* 3. 57.

the temple of their gods. Because of this insatiable lust, for as long as they thirst for gold they'll stop at nothing to obtain it.

22

Concerning the triumphal arch of Augustus:
Not far from this temple is the triumphal arch of Caesar Augustus, on which I found this inscription written:

> "Because Augustus restored a conquered world to Roman rule, regaining it for the Republic, the Roman people erected this monument;"

in other words it was a timeless memorial to record for posterity his many victories and great triumphs. The arch itself is multiple and constructed of marble, and on its stone platforms, which project outwards quite a distance, statues were placed of military commanders and those who had either distinguished themselves on campaign or fallen in the thick of battle. Among these the portrait of Augustus, larger than the others and carved with wonderful skill, is preeminent, and one can see where he triumphs and where he overcomes his foes. All over the arch there are reliefs depicting the army and cursed war, and if you look closely the battles seem very realistic. The Battle of Actium is cleverly depicted, in which Caesar, emerging from the struggle with a greater victory than he had expected, pursues Cleopatra's fleeing galley. It is captured, Cleopatra is brought before him, and after applying the asps to her breasts the proud woman, carved in Parian marble, pales on the point of death. Caesar Augustus attained the highest honours from this war, and this is how he celebrated his triumph: four white horses led by four of the most noble Romans drew a golden chariot, in which he sat, dressed in a toga embroidered with gold and jewels. In front of him stretched a long procession of captured kings, chiefs and princes, their hands bound behind their backs, along with countless other distinguished displays. His wars and achievements were spoken of in every language to be found in Rome, and the city's populace did not cease to celebrate his victory. It was even depicted in pictures, so that those who could not hear of his glory might see it. And with great celebration and indescribable joy he was led all the way to the Tarpeian rock on the Capitoline hill, where he presented both the weapons which he had borne in battle himself and those which he had captured from his enemies, hanging them up in the rotunda as a record of his great victory. There the Senate, the senatorial fathers, and the Roman people presented to him the last province, so that the fame of his triumph and the glory of his victory would be made known throughout the entire world. All these things which I have mentioned are shown in the carved reliefs on the arch.

23

I also saw several other triumphal arches, but their workmanship and carving are much the same, and the description of one can stand for them all. All of them are carved with great skill and portray to the viewer the war of a conqueror, his illustrious deeds, and the great glory of our forefathers.

24

Concerning the Arch of Pompey:

There is also the wonderful triumphal arch of Pompey the Great, built for the victory celebration after his defeat of Mithridates and his son Pharnaces. These two had fought against the Romans for forty years; they were pirates to the end, and defeated Sulla who had been sent out to deal with them, sending him packing. Pompey was despatched against them shortly thereafter, and beyond the expectation of the Romans, aided by good fortune, he completely crushed the famous Mithridates, as well as his son and their army, before a month had passed. Before returning to Rome he subjugated a large part of the East, and required it to pay tribute to Rome. He also acquired an enormous amount of gold and silver, which was displayed in a long procession at his triumph. The reliefs on his triumphal arch depict these events to the present day.

25

Concerning the triumphal column of Fabricius:

I also saw the triumphal column of Fabricius, erected by the Romans after his defeat of Pyrrhus, king of Epirus, and I don't believe there is anything higher in all of Rome. The column is round and hollow, very much like a chimney, and there are four others like it. The Romans call them marble pipes. Despite their great thickness, they give the appearance of being very slender, due to their enormous height. I have not yet managed to discover in whose honour they were raised, but when, if it pleases God, I return to [blank] from this journey, I shall take the time to investigate more diligently those things which are at the moment unclear or obscure; and I shall gladly share this research with my friends. For the moment, however, I shall stick to what I know, namely the column of the famous Fabricius. Even his enemy Pyrrhus thought well of him and praised him. After Fabricius had sent Pyrrhus's physician, a certain Philip, back to his master in chains, because he had offered to kill his master in return for payment, Pyrrhus replied to Fabricius's envoys: "Without a doubt this man is that Fabricius who can no more easily be swayed from the path of virtue than can the sun from its course." And he sent back with them the contents of his treasury, with which he had planned to buy Rome if he couldn't take it by force of arms, prompting Lucan to write:

"For which gold Fabricius did not betray you to the king."[11]

These illustrious deeds of Fabricius and many others are carved on this column.

26

Concerning the triumphal arch of Scipio:

There is also a triumphal arch of Scipio, which the Romans put up in his honour after he destroyed Hannibal. Hannibal was Rome's toughest adversary, and when the two had battled to an inconclusive draw, the Romans began to hope for the first time that they might be victorious. Hannibal had a personal demon, which advised him

---

[11] Lucan, *De bello civili* 3. 160.

to make peace with Scipio. Accordingly, a three-day truce was arranged in order to bury the dead, and Hannibal held private talks with Scipio. However, when they assembled on the fourth day, two gigantic hounds followed Hannibal to the meeting-place, and when Scipio learned of this, he refused to attend. A fierce battle ensued, and Hannibal was forced to abandon his camp. On the following day he was again beaten in a major engagement, and he took refuge with King Lircus. After being defeated yet again by Scipio, and realizing that there was no escape, he swallowed the poison which he kept in his ring, and died peacefully. Freed from their deadliest enemy, whom even today they hate and detest, the Romans spared no expense in building this triumphal arch for the victorious Scipio, and on it are carved these events and more.

27

Concerning the pyramids, which is to say the tombs of the mighty:

Now I shall add a few words about the pyramids, the tombs of the mighty, of enormous size and height, and rising to a point in the manner of a cone. The first of these which I encountered was the tomb of Romulus, which stands by the castle of Crescentius near the church of St. Peter's. The pilgrims erroneously claim that this is the grain heap of the apostle Peter, which was transformed into a stone hill of the same size when Nero confiscated it. It's an utterly worthless tale, typical of those told by pilgrims. Hidden inside every pyramid is a marble sarcophagus, with carved reliefs on all sides, in which the body of the deceased was placed.

28

Concerning the pyramid of Augustus:

Near the Porta Latina I also saw the pyramid of Augustus, constructed from square stones and held by iron clamps. These have prevented time from removing even a single stone.

29

There are many pyramids in Rome, but of all of them the one which deserves the greatest admiration is the pyramid of Julius Caesar, made of a single porphyry block. It's indeed a marvel how a block of stone of such height could have been cut, or have been raised, or remain standing; for they say that its height is 250 feet. At the top there is a bronze sphere, in which Julius Caesar's ashes and bones are deposited. Someone marvelling at it has commented:

> "If it be one stone, tell me how it was raised.
> If there be many stones, tell me where they join."

They say that it stands on the spot where a certain person encountered Julius, who was on his way to an assembly, and offered him a letter revealing the conspiracy. This warned, among other things, that he would die cruelly if he entered the assembly or the Capitol that day. Caesar took the letter, but said to the man: "At the moment I am going to speak with my astrologer, and I shall read your letter after the assembly." The astrologer was present who had predicted that Caesar would die on the first day of the month, and Caesar called to him saying: "Today is the first of the month, and I'm still alive!" The astrologer replied, "It is indeed the first day of the month, but it has not yet passed, and I hope that my prediction will be proved wrong." And immediately Caesar turned away and entered the Capitol, where he expired after receiving twenty-four stab wounds from Brutus, Cassius and their cronies. However I prefer to believe Marius Suetonius, who says that he was killed by the hilts of their swords, which left no visible wounds, and they say that because of this he was received into the company of the gods. Maro writes this as his epitaph:

> "The radiant figure marvels at the unaccustomed splendour of Olympus.
> In the woodlands I was Daphnis, known from here to the stars.
> Keeper of a handsome flock, though I was even fairer,"[12]

and so forth. In his left hand they found the letter warning him of the conspiracy. And so Caesar, lord and master of the world, who

---

[12] Virgil, *Eclogues* 5. 56, 43-44.

assumed power after first suppressing liberty, now reposes in this bronze sphere, his body reduced to ashes. The pilgrims call this pyramid "St. Peter's needle," and they make great efforts to crawl underneath it, where the stone rests on four bronze lions, claiming falsely that those who manage to do so are cleansed from their sins having made a true penance.

30

Concerning the lighthouse at Alexandria:

Another great wonder is the Alexandrian lighthouse, which stands in the sea on four crabs made of glass. One wonders how such enormous crabs could have been manufactured of glass, how they could be placed in the sea without being broken, and how the cement foundations supported by the crabs could survive underwater. It is also puzzling how the cement hardened underwater, why the crabs are not broken in the sea, and why the foundation doesn't slip under the great weight of cement. Isidore[13] describes a type of sand which has this property: if it is mixed with water, subjected to sun or to fire, reduced to its original sandy state, and then plunged into water, it solidifies and turns to stone. But it's not my task to explain miracles.

31

I shall not bother to discuss the Colosseum, the palace of Titus and Vespasian, for words are inadequate to describe its size and ingenious construction. Adjoining this structure is a statue of the sow which Aeneas is said to have found giving birth. According to the prediction of Helenus, Priam's son, it was a sign that the city should be built on that spot, since the Fates had decreed that it would rule the entire world. About this statue Virgil wrote:

> "A sow found under the oak trees,
> Lying white on the ground, and white the offspring around her teats."[14]

---

[13] Cf. Isidore of Seville, *Etymologiae* 16.i.8.
[14] Virgil, *Aeneid* 8. 43, 45.

This statue has been skillfully carved from the most brilliant Parian marble, and there are thirty suckling piglets.

32

In the portico in front of the winter palace of the lord pope there is a bronze statue of the she-wolf which is supposed to have suckled Romulus and Remus. But this is indeed a tall tale! "Wolf" was a woman of extraordinary beauty who lived in Rome in ancient times, and when she found Romulus and Remus cast into the Tiber, she nourished them as her own. She was called "Wolf" because her beauty and enticements caused men to be seized with lust for her. This bronze wolf stalks a bronze ram, which also stands in front of the palace, and from its mouth water pours for washing one's hands. Water for handwashing used to run from the wolf's teats, but now its feet are broken and it has been removed from its original place.

33

In front of it there is a bronze tablet, called the tablet "prohibiting sin," on which are written the principal statutes of the law. On this tablet I read much, but understood little, for they were aphorisms, and the reader has to supply most of the words.

Commentary

ABBREVIATIONS

The sources most frequently cited in the commentary have been abbreviated as follows:

Cod. topog.   R. Valentini and G. Zucchetti, *Codice topografico della città di Roma* 4 vols. (Rome 1940-1953).

M.R. James   M.R James, "Magister Gregorius de Mirabilibus urbis Romae," *English Historical Review* 32 (1917), 531-554.

Migne, PG   *Patrologiae cursus completus, series Graeca*, ed. J.P. Migne, 161 vols. (Paris 1857-1866).

Migne, PL   *Patrologiae cursus completus, series Latina*, ed. J.P. Migne, 217 vols. (Paris 1844-1855).

Platner-Ashby   Samuel Platner and Thomas Ashby, *A Topographical Dictionary of Ancient Rome* (London 1929).

G. Rushforth   G. Rushforth, "Magister Gregorius de Mirabilibus urbis Romae: a New Description of Rome in the Twelfth Century," *Journal of Roman Studies* 9 (1919), 14-58.

1

The *Narracio* opens with Gregory's recollection of his first view of the city, seen from the slope of a hill. Presumably this is Monte Mario or another of the hills behind the Vatican, which would be traversed by travellers either following the right bank of the Tiber or approaching from the coast on the via Aurelia. The alternative for those using the via Cassia would have been to cross the river at the Milvian bridge, a few kilometres above the city, and then enter through the porta Flaminia, but this route does not provide any panoramic view. He speaks of a forest of towers ("seges turrium"), and indeed the city possessed many hundreds of these in the Middle Ages, mostly rising above domestic habitations as secure places of refuge in times of civic strife.[1]

The chapter is rich in quotations, beginning with three from Lucan's *De bello civili*, an unfinished epic poem in ten books which takes as its theme the civil war between Julius Caesar and the Roman Senate. A number of medieval copies of this work survive, and Gregory either had such a manuscript at hand or else knew the text well. The chapter concludes with his only quotation from a near-contemporary source, the poem "Par tibi, Roma" of Hildebert of Lavardin.[2]

2

Gregory states that there are fourteen gates, and he then lists fourteen names. However, two of these are by his own admission identical (porta Aquileia = St. Lawrence), and furthermore they are the same as a third (porta Tiburtina), thus reducing the actual total to twelve. Of these, nine can be identified, while three (Sacra, Marcia, Livia) are unknown from other sources. Either they refer to gates not otherwise mentioned by Gregory (e.g. the Praenestina or the Ostiensis), or else they are fabrications. It is possible that he remembered the number of gates which he had seen (14), but not all of their names, and thus had to improvise. Alternatively, he may have remembered the number 14 from the enumeration of the gates in some other source which he had read, but did not have that text (and consequently the list) at hand. There are a number of possible candidates in this regard. In his account of the sixth-century Gothic wars, Procopius of Caesarea states that Rome has fourteen gates (5.xix.1), although he does not name them. The Einsiedeln Itinerary, compiled in the late eighth or

---

[1] For the towers of medieval Rome see Emma Amadei, *Le Torri di Roma*, 3rd ed. (Rome 1969), and Aino Katermaa, "Le casetorri medievali di Roma," *Opuscula Instituti Romani Finlandiae* I (1981), 41-55.

[2] See Introduction, n. 20.

early ninth century, lists fourteen gates by name.¹ The same fourteen, although with some minor variations in nomenclature, are listed in the *Gesta Regum Anglorum* of William of Malmesbury, immediately following the text of Hildebert's "Par tibi, Roma."² If it was through William that Gregory knew these lines, then this may also have been his source of information concerning the number of gates. The issue is complicated by the fact that Gregory does not present his list of names in any apparent order, unlike most of the other medieval sources which proceed either clockwise (e.g. both the Einsiedeln Itinerary and William of Malmesbury) or counterclockwise (e.g. the *Mirabilia*) around the city's perimeter. The *Mirabilia* is unusual in that it lists not fourteen but fifteen, specifying that there are twelve for the main part of the city and three for Trastevere. The extra gate belongs to the latter zone: the porta Septimiana.³

1. Aurea: This is the Porta Aurelia on the Janiculum hill, on the site of the modern gate of San Pancrazio.⁴ It marked the beginning of the via Aurelia, which followed the coast through Pisa and Genoa to southern France. The corruption from "Aurelia" to "Aurea" was common in the Middle Ages, and both forms are given in the *Mirabilia*: "porta Aurelia vel Aurea." The present gate was erected by Pius IX in 1854, its predecessor having been severely damaged during the fighting of June 1849.

2. Latina: This is presumably identical to the modern Porta Latina, although there is some doubt as to which gate Gregory intended since he later identifies the Porta Ostiensis by this name (ch. 28), and the Ostiensis is omitted from the present list.⁵

---

²⁻¹ *Cod. topog.* 2: 202-207.
² William of Malmesbury, *Gesta Regum Anglorum* 4. 2, where a description of Rome is included by the author in his account of the First Crusade in the year 1097. William's source of this information, as yet unidentified, is considered on the basis of internal evidence to date from the seventh century. For a discussion see Patrick Sims-Williams, "William of Malmesbury and 'La Silloge Epigrafica di Cambridge'," *Archivum Historiae Pontificae* 21 (1983), 9-33, esp. 31-33.
³ *Mirabilia*, cap. 2 (*Cod. topog.* 3: 17-18). For more detailed information on the history of the walls and the gates see Ian Richmond, *The City Wall of Imperial Rome* (Oxford 1930), and Malcolm Todd, *The Walls of Rome* (London 1978).
⁴ Platner-Ashby, p. 404.
⁵ *Ibid.*, pp. 408-409 (Latina) and pp. 410-411 (Ostiensis).

3. Sacra: Unidentified. There is no apparent connection between this name and any of the gates which Gregory omits from his list.

4. Salaria: The ancient Porta Salaria, which gave access to the road of the same name, was damaged in the assault of Rome in 1870, and replaced in 1873. This new gate was demolished in 1921. It stood on the site of the present Piazza Fiume.[6]

5. Marcia: Unidentified. Rushforth suggested that it "might be a corruption of 'Maior',"[7] but suspected that Gregory had invented the name in order to fill out his list. If this was the case, he may have obtained the idea from one of the principal aqueducts, the Aqua Marcia, constructed in 144-140 BC by the praetor Q. Marcius Rex. This crossed the Aurelian wall in the porta Tiburtina.[8]

6. Livia: also unidentified.

7. Collatina: There is no known gate by this name. Gregory may be referring to one of the northern entrances in the wall around the Leonine city, adjoining the Castel Sant' Angelo, which is called the Porta Cornelia by William of Malmesbury and the Porta Collina in the *Mirabilia*, or perhaps he has in mind the Porta Collina of the older Servian wall.[9] The only other source to give Gregory's alternative is John Capgrave's fifteenth-century work, *Ye Solace of Pilgrims*, which may itself have been influenced by a reading of Gregory.[10] A more likely possibility is that Gregory borrowed the name from the via Collatina, a country road of no great importance which joined the via Tiburtina just outside the Aurelian walls.[11] He does seem to have been particularly familiar with this area of the city, which leads one to suspect that he may have been lodged in the vicinity.

8. Flaminia: The manuscript in St. Catharine's College erroneously gives "flammea." The Flaminian gate, now known as the Porta del

---

[6] *Ibid.*, p. 416.
[7] G. Rushforth, p. 20.
[8] Platner-Ashby, pp. 24-25.
[9] For this last suggestion see Rushforth, p. 20, and Platner-Ashby, p. 406.
[10] G. Rushforth, p. 20.
[11] See T. Ashby, "The Classical Topography of the Roman Campagna — I," *Papers of the British School at Rome* 1 (1902), 125-285, esp. 138-139, and Lorenzo Quilici, "La via Collatina: analisi topografico dell' antico percorso," *Bullettino della Commissione Archeologica Comunale di Roma* 79 (1963-64), 99-106.

COMMENTARY, CH. 2   41

Popolo, was one of the most important entrances to the city from the north. The Normans under Robert Guiscard had entered Rome by this gate in 1084.[12]

9. Numantia: Presumably the Porta Nomentana, which was walled up by Pope Pius IV in 1564 and replaced by the Porta Pia.[13]

10. Appia: The entrance from the via Appia, now called the Porta S. Sebastiano because it leads to the important suburban church of that name.[14]

11.-13. Tiburtina: The manuscript reads "Tirburtina". This is the gate from which a road led to Tibur (Tivoli).[15] From the gate a covered portico followed the road as far as the complex of churches and monasteries at the shrine of St. Lawrence (S. Lorenzo fuori le mura),[16] hence its alternate name "Porta S. Lorenzo." This is the only alternate name which is mentioned by Gregory, and he mistakenly links it not with the Tiburtina but with the next gate in his list, the "Porta Aquileia." This is puzzling. "Aquileia" may be yet another name for the same gate, or perhaps Gregory has become muddled and has placed his phrase "que nunc sancti Laurentii dicitur" in the wrong place. If it is a third name for the Porta Tiburtina, it is not one used elsewhere, although it is remarkably similar to the "Porta Aequilia" which is given as an alternate name to the Porta Labicana by the mid-fourteenth-century author, Giovanni Cavallini de Cerronibus.[17] There is no apparent connection to the city of Aquileia in northern Italy. Rushforth has suggested that the name may be a corruption of "Porta Esquilina," the corresponding gate in the Servian wall.[18] If the name is indeed a corruption, it may well have come from the Aqua Iulia, one of the three aqueducts which crossed the via Tiburtina in this gateway. However, in the light of Gregory's

---

[12] Platner-Ashby, pp. 407-408.
[13] Ibid., p. 410.
[14] Ibid., pp. 402-403.
[15] Ibid., pp. 417-418.
[16] See L. Reekmans, "L'implantation monumentale chrétienne dans la zone suburbaine de Rome du IVe au IXe siècle," *Rivista di Archeologia Cristiana* 44 (1968), 173-207, esp. 195-198.
[17] Giovanni Cavallini de Cerronibus, *Polistoria de virtutibus et dotibus Romanorum*, see *Cod. topog.* 4: 11-54, esp. 32.
[18] Rushforth, p. 20.

evident uncertainty on the matter of the gates, it is difficult to guess what he intended. Curiously, the *Mirabilia* also gives three names for the gate: "porta Taurina, quae dicitur Sancti Laurentii, vel Tiburtina." The first of these names comes from the carved *bucrania* on each side of the aqueduct arch, as is explained by Giovanni Cavallini de Cerronibus.[19]

14. Asinaria: The gate in the Aurelian wall adjoining the church of S. Giovanni in Laterano, and the entrance to the city used in AD 536 by the Byzantine general Belisarius.[20]

3

The "castrum Crescentii" is the Castel Sant' Angelo, constructed in the second century AD as the mausoleum of the emperor Hadrian and subsequently converted into a fortress.[1] The identification of the structure with Crescentius stems from the tenth-century occupation of the castle by an important Roman family of this name. From this stronghold they led the local opposition to the transalpine Holy Roman Emperors, until Iohannes Crescentius was captured and beheaded by Otto III in 998.[2] The building is referred to by this title in a variety of twelfth-century sources.[3]

Although there is now no trace of the bronze bull which seemed so lifelike to Gregory, there is no reason to doubt his statement that such a statue once stood on one of the battlements, and indeed its

---

[19] *Cod. topog.* 4: 33: "Porta Taurina dicta est ab olim a capitibus taurorum, supra portam huius modi sculptis, in ingressu et exitu dictae portae ..."

[20] Platner-Ashby, p. 404.

[3.1] For a synopsis of the structure's history see Platner-Ashby, pp. 336-338.

[2] For a summary of this struggle see Cesare d'Onofrio, *Castel S. Angelo e Borgo tra Roma e Papato* (Rome 1978), pp. 182-189.

[3] In addition to Gregory (who repeats it in ch. 27), this appellation appears in the *Mirabilia* (*Cod. topog.* 3: 23) and the *Ordo* of Cencio Savelli (*Cod. topog.* 3: 224). It may also be found in the description of Rome *circa* AD 1154 by Nikolas, abbot of Munkathvera in Iceland, see F.P. Magoun, "The Rome of Two Northern Pilgrims: Archbishop Sigeric of Canterbury and Abbot Nikolas of Munkathvera," *Harvard Theological Review* 33 (1940), 267-289. For this and other medieval terms for the structure see Carlo Cecchelli, "Per la storia antica e medioevale di Castel S. Angelo," *Archivio della Società Romana di Storia Patria* 74 (1951), 27-67.

presence there is also recorded in descriptions of the castle in the *Mirabilia* and the *Graphia aureae urbis*, which mention bronze peacocks and four horses in addition to the bull.[4] The sixth-century historian Procopius noted that the walls of the fortress were adorned with a number of marble statues of men and horses, some of which were taken down by the defending garrison in AD 537 and used as ammunition against the besieging Ostrogoths.[5] The bronze pieces, less easily dislodged or broken, presumably survived that occasion.

Bronze statues of bulls were also to be found elsewhere in Rome, and Procopius mentions one which stood by a fountain in the Forum of Peace.[6] The *Mirabilia* also reports that two gilded bronze bulls decorated the Pantheon.[7] Among the pieces in the Palazzo dei Conservatori collection is the hindquarters of a colossal bronze bull which was found in the Vicolo delle Palme (Trastevere) in 1850,[8] but it seems unlikely that this could have been the animal seen by Gregory. His bull, like so many of Rome's ancient bronzes, probably ended its days in the melting pot, although two peacocks from the Castel Sant' Angelo do survive and may be found in the Cortile della Pigna of the Vatican Museum.[9] The legend ("fabula"), with which Gregory seems to assume that his readers are familiar, is of course that of the Rape of Europa, probably best known in the Middle Ages from Ovid's *Metamorphoses*.[10] Gregory was certainly familiar with this work, since he later quotes from it (ch. 19).

4-5

This monument, which seems to have particularly attracted the attention of our author since he devotes more space to it than to any other, is the well-known equestrian bronze statue of the emperor Marcus Aurelius (AD 161-180). In 1538 the statue was moved to the Capitoline hill by order of Pope Paul III, where it would become the centrepiece of

---

[4] *Cod. topog.* 3: 46, 86.
[5] Procopius of Caesarea, *History of the Wars* 5.xxii.14, 22-23.
[6] *Ibid.*, 8.xxi.12.
[7] *Cod. topog.* 3: 48.
[8] The find is reported and discussed in the *Bullettino dell' Instituto di Corrispondenza Archeologica* (1850), 33, 110-112.
[9] These had already been removed to the atrium of St. Peter's by the twelfth century, cf. *Cod. topog.* 3: 46.
[10] Ovid, *Metamorphoses* 2.833-875.

Michelangelo's design for the Campidoglio; and there it remained until recent years, apart from a brief period during World War II.[1] In the aftermath of the April 1979 bomb explosion in the square, the Istituto Centrale del Restauro was asked to examine the statue's physical condition, and their report drew attention to the severe corrosion of the metal which had resulted from exposure to atmospheric pollution.[2] As a result of the Istituto's findings, the statue was removed from the Campidoglio in January 1981, and it seems likely that the original will now be housed in a more protected environment. Its place on the Capitoline will probably be taken by a replica, as has been done with the bronze horses on the façade of San Marco in Venice.

In the Middle Ages the monument stood where Gregory saw it, in front of the papal palace at the Lateran ("ante palatium domni pape"). The first source to refer to it in this location is the *Liber Pontificalis*, in its biographies of two tenth-century pontiffs, John XIII (965-972) and John XIV (983-984).[3] These passages suggest that the spot was used for the public exposure of the bodies of executed criminals and other malefactors. It seems likely, however, that the figure was already in place by the end of the eighth century, when it prompted Charlemagne to import an equestrian bronze statue from Ravenna to stand before his "Lateran" palace at Aachen,[4] and to commission a bronze statuette of himself on horseback (now in the Musée du Louvre, Paris). This was by no means the only occasion on which it would influence artists and patrons of subsequent eras. The bronze miniature by Antonio Filarete (now in Dresden) is thought

---

[4-1] For the statue and its movements see G. Zucchetti, "Marco Aurelio," *Capitolium* 28 (1953), 328-332; J.S. Ackerman, "Marcus Aurelius on the Capitoline Hill," *Renaissance News* 10 (1957), 69-75; and Philip Fehl, "The Placement of the Equestrian Statue of Marcus Aurelius in the Middle Ages," *Journal of the Warburg and Courtauld Institutes* 37 (1974), 362-367.

[2] See Eugenio La Rocca "Sulle vicende del Marco Aurelio dal 1912 al 1980," *Studi Romani* 29 (1981), 56-60.

[3] *Liber Pontificalis*, ed. L. Duchesne (Paris 1886) 2: 252, 259.

[4] As recorded by the ninth-century Ravenna historian, Agnellus, in his *Liber Pontificalis Ecclesiae Ravennatis*: see *Monumenta Germaniae Historica. Scriptores Rerum Langobardicarum et Italicarum* (Hannover 1878), 338. See also Richard Krautheimer, "The Carolingian Revival of Early Christian Architecture," *Art Bulletin* 24 (1942), 1-38, esp. 35-36.

to be one of the first miniature reproductions of classical objects in the Renaissance,[5] and replicas of this type would become widely popular in the sixteenth century. Other artists were similarly inspired, and the statue appears for example in the "Triumph of Thomas Aquinas," painted by Filippino Lippi in the church of S. Maria sopra Minerva in Rome. In 1474 the equestrian figure had been set up on a pedestal by Pope Sixtus IV, and this setting is recorded both in the Lippi fresco and in a drawing by Martin van Heemskerck (Kupferstichkabinett, Berlin).[6]

Gregory first records two popular opinions concerning the identity of the rider: Theodoric (king of the Ostrogoths, and of Italy, in the early sixth century), and Constantine (Roman emperor, AD 306-337). The latter possibility appears to have enjoyed a wider circulation. The monument is referred to as the "caballum Constantini" in both *Liber Pontificalis* passages, and is similarly identified in a variety of other medieval sources, including the twelfth-century description of Rome by Benjamin of Tudela.[7] This must have seemed an obvious choice for an imperial statue at the Lateran, the site which Constantine had donated to the church shortly after his occupation of Rome in AD 312, and it was probably his widespread fame as the first emperor to have embraced Christianity which in later years saved the statue from the melting pot. It is the only equestrian monument to have survived from antiquity. There was in fact an equestrian statue of Constantine in Rome, located in the Forum. This is first mentioned in the fourth-century *Notitia urbis Romae regionum XIIII*,[8] and it also appears twice in the eighth-century Einsiedeln Itinerary.[9] Its fate is unknown.

In the fifteenth century, the identification of the statue outside the Lateran palace sparked considerable interest among humanist scholars,

---

[5] Francis Haskell and Nicholas Penny, *Taste and the Antique* (New Haven 1981), p. 252.

[6] Published by Fehl, pls. 80a and 80b.

[7] Francis Nichols, *The Marvels of Rome* (London 1889), p. 156. See also Paul Borchardt, "The Sculpture in Front of the Lateran as Described by Benjamin of Tudela and Magister Gregorius," *Journal of Roman Studies* 26 (1936), 68-70.

[8] *Cod. topog.* 1: 173.

[9] *Cod. topog.* 2: 177, 192. See also E. Babut, "Les statues équestres du Forum," *Mélanges d'Archéologie et d'Histoire* 20 (1900), 209-222.

who began to compare the rider's face to effigies on antique coins and medals. The first to propose the name of Marcus Aurelius seems to have been Bartolomeo Sacchi da Piadena (better known as "il Platina"), in his biography of Pope Sixtus IV,[10] and subsequently this identification has found general acceptance. Lauer's suggestion that the piece may have originally stood in the emperor's family home, on the Celian hill adjoining the Lateran,[11] has been strengthened by recent excavations at this site, beneath the medieval hospital of St. Andrew, which revealed the base of a large monument. Its dimensions correspond exactly to the base of the Marcus Aurelius.[12]

Dismissing the "vanas fabulas" of the "peregrini" and the "populus Romanus," Gregory then offers his readers two possible explanations for the statue, both acquired from "cardinales et clerici Romane curie." The first involves an attack on Rome by the king of the Miseni. The magic powers of this king prevent the Romans from using their weapons against him, but the city is saved when a courageous soldier named Marcus captures the enemy king and tramples him to death beneath the hoofs of his horse. At Marcus's request, a monument is then erected to record the deed for posterity, with the dwarf king placed where he fell, beneath the horse's feet. It is indeed plausible that a figure of a fallen enemy was originally included in the group, but no trace of it has survived.

This story is remarkably similar to the account in the *Mirabilia*, which also begins by warning its readers that, while the statue is commonly said to represent the emperor Constantine, in fact it depicts

---

[10] Bartolomeo Platina, *Liber de vita Christi ac omnium pontificum* published in *Rerum Italicarum Scriptores*, ed. L. A. Muratori, nuova ed., t. 3, par. 1, 418: "Et ne monumenta aeternae Urbis perirent, equum illum aeneum vetustate quassum, et iam collabentem cum sessore M. Aurelio Antonino, restituit, quem ante aedem Constantinianae basilicae cernimus." See also the discussion by G.B. De Rossi and G. Gatti, "Miscellanea di notizie bibliografiche e critiche per la topografia e la storia dei monumenti di Roma," *Bullettino della Commissione Archeologica Comunale di Roma* 14 (1886), 240-247, 345-356, esp. 348-352; and G. Zucchetti, pp. 331-332.
[11] Philippe Lauer, *Le Palais de Latran* (Paris 1911), pp. 22-23.
[12] The discovery is published by V. Santa Maria Scrinari, "Scavi sotto sala Mazzoni all' ospedale di S. Giovanni in Roma. Relazione preliminare," *Atti della Pontificia Accademia Romana di Archeologia. Rendiconti* 41 (1968-1969), 167-189, esp. 179-180.

someone else.[13] It then relates how the city was once attacked by an eastern king, and how it was saved when he was captured by a certain warrior ("quidam armiger"). There is no mention of this hero's name, nor are the attackers identified; and in this version the soldier offers his services in return for a handsome reward, whereas the services of Gregory's Marcus were solicited by the Romans. Both accounts include a bird, which signals the presence of the enemy king: in the *Narracio* a cuckoo ("cuculus"), but in the *Mirabilia* a species of owl ("cocovaia"). This was no doubt intended to explain the bird which medieval viewers of the bronze monument believed they saw perched on the horse's head between its ears.[14] The origin of this legend is not known, although Rushforth has suggested that it may stem from an account of the great victory won by Marcus Licinius Crassus in Moesia in 29 BC, in the course of which the consul personally defeated and killed the enemy chieftain.[15] Although some imagination is required to stretch "Miseni" into "Moesi," no better alternative comes to mind.

The second possibility which Gregory relates (ch. 5) is more easily explained. The citizen who sacrifices his own life, mounting his horse and leaping into the pestilential chasm in order that the city might be spared, is none other than Marcus Curtius, whose story is told by the Roman historian Livy.[16] Again there is a parallel tale in the *Mirabilia*, which in describing the Roman Forum speaks of a place known as "Infernus," where an unnamed Roman soldier threw himself into an opening, thus saving the city.[17] The *Graphia aureae urbis*, whose compiler was evidently better informed, identifies Marcus Curtius by name.[18] The name supplied by Gregory is rather puzzling: Quintus Quirinus. It is interesting to note that the only subsequent medieval writer to make use of the *Narracio*, Ranulph Higden in his

---

[13] *Mirabilia* (cap. 15): "caballus aereus qui dicitur Constantini, sed ita non est," (*Cod. topog.* 3: 32). The *Mirabilia* story is repeated in the *Graphia aureae urbis* (*Cod. topog.* 3: 91-92).

[14] This bird may be nothing more than a fanciful interpretation of a tuft of hair; see Zucchetti, p. 329, and Fehl, p. 367.

[15] Rushforth, p. 22.

[16] Livy, *Ab urbe condita* 7.vi.1-6.

[17] *Mirabilia*, cap. 24 (*Cod. topog.* 3: 56).

[18] *Cod. topog.* 3: 90.

Polychronicon (cf. Introduction), gives the name as Quintus Curtius.[19] This is half-way to Livy's original, and it would be useful to know whether Higden copied the name from his manuscript of the *Narracio* or took it upon himself to make a correction. One suspects that the scribe of the extant Cambridge manuscript may have made a copying error, although the name does appear in the text four times.

Gregory is apparently the only medieval author to link the Marcus Curtius legend with the Lateran statue, and the attempt to account for the presence of the dwarf is aptly described by M.R. James as "very awkward."[20] However, he is only reporting the stories which he has heard from the best educated scholars at the papal court ("quam a senioribus et cardinalibus et viris doctissimis didici"), and cannot be faulted for their inaccuracy. No indication is given of which explanation he personally prefers.

The role of Pope Gregory I (590-604), who is here held responsible for dismantling the monument in its original location on the Capitoline, will be examined in the commentary on chapter six. It should be noted, however, that there are four antique gilded bronze columns in the Lateran basilica, and it may well be these which our author had in mind.[21]

6

The colossal bronze head and hand, the latter holding an orb, which Gregory observed on columns outside the Lateran palace, survive today in the Palazzo dei Conservatori museum on the Capitoline. They were among the bronzes donated to the Roman people by Pope Sixtus IV in December of 1471.[1] The original statue was clearly that of an emperor, and although his precise identity has not yet been

---

[19] Ranulph Higden, *Polychronicon*, ed. C. Babington (London 1865), 1: 228, 232.

[20] M.R. James, p. 540.

[21] See Rushforth, pp. 21-22, and Fehl, p. 366.

[6.1] For Sixtus IV's donation see W.S. Heckscher, *Sixtus IIII Aeneas Insignes Statuas Romano Populo Restituendas Censuit* (The Hague 1955); and T. Buddensieg, "Die Statuenstiftung Sixtus' IV. im Jahre 1471," *Römisches Jahrbuch für Kunstgeschichte* 20 (1983), 33-73.

COMMENTARY, CH. 6   49

determined, it is probably Constantine or one of his fourth-century successors.[2] The hand and orb are now separated, but it is not known when this was done. They were still together in the mid fifteenth century, since they appear intact in an illustration to Johannes Marcanova's *Quaedam antiquitatum fragmenta* (composed *circa* 1465).[3] Gregory identifies the fragments as coming from a statue which represented either the Sun or the city of Rome. Clearly he has in mind the famous Colossus which, according to Suetonius (Nero xxxi), was set up by the emperor Nero in the vestibule of the Domus Aurea.[4] Pliny (*Natural History* 34. 45) attributes it to the artist Zenodorus. After Nero's death, it was converted into a statue of the Sun by Vespasian. In the early second century, Hadrian moved it closer to the Flavian amphitheatre, in order to create space for his Temple of Venus and Rome, and in the Middle Ages the amphitheatre may have come to be called the "Colosseum" as a result of the statue's proximity.[5] The eventual fate of the Colossus is not known. It appears on coins of the third-century emperor, Gordian III,[6] and is mentioned in the catalogues of the fourth century.[7] It must have been pulled

---

[2] *A Catalogue of the Ancient Sculptures preserved in the Municipal Collections of Rome. The Sculptures of the Palazzo dei Conservatori*, ed. H. Stuart Jones (Oxford 1926), p. 173, identifies it as "probably" Constans I (337-350) on the basis of comparisons to coin effigies, although Constantine and Constantius II (337-361) have also been suggested. Heckscher, p. 14, suggests that Constantius II brought the statue to Rome for his triumph in AD 357.

[3] The illustrations accompanying the text in the Modena copy of this work have been attributed to Cyriac of Ancona by C. Huelsen, *La Roma Antica di Ciriaco d'Ancona* (Rome 1907). For the drawing with the head and hand see esp. pp. 28-29 and tav. VII. The Modena drawings served as models for a second illustrated copy, now in the Princeton University Library (MS Garrett 158), see Elizabeth Lawrence, "The Illustrations of the Garrett and Modena Manuscripts of Marcanova," *Memoirs of the American Academy in Rome* 6 (1927), 127-131.

[4] Platner-Ashby, p. 130; Jean Gagé, "Le Colosse et la fortune de Rome," *Mélanges d'Archéologie et d'Histoire* 45 (1928), 106-122.

[5] This is argued by Huelsen, "Note di topografia romana antica e medievale," *Bullettino della Commissione Archeologica Comunale di Roma* 54 (1926), 49-66, esp. 53-64, but opposed by Howard Canter, "The Venerable Bede and the Colosseum," *Transactions and Proceedings of the American Philological Association* 61 (1930), 150-164.

[6] See E. Nash, *Pictorial Dictionary of Ancient Rome* 1 (Tübingen 1961), fig. 317.

[7] *Cod. topog.* 1: 100.

down long before the twelfth century, by which time some of the city's inhabitants had not unreasonably transferred the association to the pieces outside the Lateran. The *Narracio* is not the only source to make this link. It is repeated in the *Graphia aureae urbis* (which speaks of the Colossus "cuius caput et manus nunc sunt ante Lateranum"),[8] a fourteenth-century edition of the *Mirabilia*,[9] and a variety of other texts.[10] Popular imagination, however, also incorporated a rather different view, believing the pieces to come from a statue of the Old Testament hero Samson. This may be found, for example, in the description of the Lateran statues made by Rabbi Benjamin ben Jonah of Tudela, who visited the city in the year 1166, and Paul Borchardt has suggested that the identification may stem from the deep eye sockets, which could have given the impression of blindness.[11] Rushforth is undoubtedly correct in believing that Gregory's statement about the statue revolving with the sun stems from Suetonius's description (Nero xxxi) of the revolving roof in the principal banquet room of the Domus Aurea.[12]

The *Narracio* attributes the destruction of the Colossus to Pope Gregory I (590-604), one of the better-known early medieval pontiffs, whose books and pastoral letters enjoyed a wide circulation in subsequent centuries. In chapter four, Pope Gregory was assigned the responsibility for having dismantled the equestrian monument on the Capitoline, in order to use its bronze support columns in the Lateran basilica. Now the charge is somewhat different: the deliberate demolition of pagan idols, a view which will be again stated at the beginning of chapter twelve. Our author clearly believes that his namesake played a major role in the process of Christianizing the city through the eradication of vestiges of the pagan past. With specific reference to Nero's Colossus, the *Narracio* differs in this regard from other medieval topographical texts. The earliest version of the *Mirabilia*, and also the *Graphia aureae urbis*, are silent on

[8] *Cod. topog.* 3: 90.
[9] *Ibid.*, 3: 195-196.
[10] Among them the anonymous fifteenth-century *Tractatus de rebus antiquis et situ urbis Romae* (*Cod. topog.* 4: 132).
[11] Paul Borchardt, "The Sculpture in Front of the Lateran as Described by Benjamin of Tudela and Magister Gregorius," *Journal of Roman Studies* 25 (1936), 68-70.
[12] Rushforth, p. 23.

COMMENTARY, CH. 6 51

the question of responsibility, but a later edition of the *Mirabilia* is more explicit, giving credit for the act to an earlier pontiff, Sylvester I (314-325), the contemporary of the emperor Constantine.[13] Sylvester is also named in this regard in the anonymous fifteenth-century *Tractatus de rebus antiquis et situ urbis Romae*.[14] There are, however, parallels for the *Narracio* in a more general sense. As has been noted in the Introduction, the twelfth-century English historian, John of Salisbury, attributed to Pope Gregory the destruction of the pagan library on the Palatine, and this view (that it was Pope Gregory who was chiefly responsible for removing pagan statues) may be found in a variety of late medieval texts.[15] As a result, his memory would be villified by sixteenth-century humanists. Although no other authors specifically link his name with the destruction of the Colossus, they do speak in general terms of the amputation of heads and limbs,[16] and it is no doubt this particular aspect of the Gregory legend which led the author of the *Narracio* to connect the pope with the severed head and hand at the Lateran.

In this chapter we find the first use of the anonymous medieval text entitled *De septem miraculis mundi*,[17] from which Gregory has

[13] *Cod. topog.* 3: 196.
[14] *Cod. topog.* 4: 132.
[15] See Tilmann Buddensieg, "Gregory the Great, the Destroyer of Pagan Idols. The History of a Medieval Legend Concerning the Decline of Ancient Art and Literature," *Journal of the Warburg and Courtauld Institutes* 28 (1965), 44-65; and *idem*, "Criticism of Ancient Architecture in the Sixteenth and Seventeenth Centuries," in *Classical Influences on European Culture, A.D. 1500-1700*, ed. R. Bolgar (Cambridge 1976), pp. 335-348, esp. 344. It seems likely that a certain amount of deliberate destruction did indeed take place in the early Middle Ages. Byzantine hagiographical texts frequently include similar stories, see Cyril Mango "Antique Statuary and the Byzantine Beholder," *Dumbarton Oaks Papers* 17 (1963), 53-75.
[16] For example Giovanni Cavallini de Cerronibus *circa* 1350: "Et ideo ymaginibus daemonum capita atque membra Gregorius primus papa, natione Romanus, fecit generaliter amputari, ut per hoc extyrpata radice haereticae pravitatis, palma ecclesiasticae veritatis plenius exaltaretur, secundum Cronicas." (*Cod. topog.* 4: 44).
[17] For this text see H. Omont, "Les sept merveilles du monde au moyen âge," *Bibliothèque de l'École des Chartes* 43 (1882), 40-59; and M. Demus-Quatember, "Zur Weltwunderliste des Pseudo-Beda und ihren Beziehungen zu Rom," *Römische Historische Mitteilungen* 12 (1970), 67-92. It is interesting to note from Omont's list of manuscripts that the text enjoyed a wide circulation in north-western Europe, and thus there is little surprise that Gregory should know it.

derived the original height of the Colossus[18] and the information that it stood on the island of "Herodius." This last is of course a corruption of "Rhodes." It is difficult to know precisely what the author intended, but clearly he believed that the Colossus which is described in the *De septem miraculis mundi* is the same statue from which the Lateran pieces were taken. It is less certain whether he interprets the phrase "insula Herodii" as meaning an island in the usual sense, or whether, as Rushforth suggests, he uses it in its other sense as a large block of buildings.[19] Some interesting light has been shed on Gregory's use of this medieval account of the seven wonders of the world as a result of Margarete Demus-Quatember's recent study of a sixteenth-century painting by Martin van Heemskerck. The work in question, now in the collection of the Walters Art Gallery in Baltimore, consists principally of a fantastic view of the city of Rome, in which a number of these seven wonders can be identified. Since it seems unlikely that Heemskerck can have based his painting on Gregory's *Narracio*, it would appear that there must have existed a version of the *De septem miraculis mundi* in which the wonders were associated with the city of Rome. If such a version did exist (and it is otherwise rather difficult to account for the Baltimore painting), and if Gregory knew it, then his inclusion in the *Narracio* of six of the seven wonders is more readily explained.[20]

The political significance of the hand holding the orb, representing dominion over the entire world, is not lost on Gregory, and it was possibly for this very reason that the piece was originally brought to the Lateran to be part of the papal collection.[21] However, his careful explanation of why the left hand should hold the sword, and the right hand the orb, is puzzling since the hand now in the Palazzo dei Conservatori is a left hand not a right. This is indeed what might

---

[18] Suetonius records the height as 120 ft., and Pliny as 106.5 or 119 ft., depending on the manuscript.

[19] Rushforth, p. 23.

[20] See M. Demus-Quatember, "Ricordo di Roma. Mirabilia urbis Romae und Miracula Mundi auf einem Gemälde von Martin van Heemskerck," *Römische Historische Mitteilungen* 25 (1983), 203-223, esp. 218-219.

[21] Heckscher (p. 46) believes that this was done "most likely in the course of the eighth-century Constantinian revival."

be expected, since it is normal in Roman imperial portraiture for the orb to be held in the left hand.

7

Very few medieval sources mention the boy extracting the thorn from his foot which, like the pieces of the colossal statue just described, formed part of the 1471 donation of Pope Sixtus IV. It too is now in the Palazzo dei Conservatori collection. Gregory is unique in his bizarre identification of the statue as representing the god Priapus, but if indeed it was set up on a column like its companions, and if one had to "look up" at it as he suggests, then the genitals would appear as a prominent feature. The "Spinario" or "Thorn-plucker" type may be found frequently in both Byzantine and western European art of the Middle Ages, and in the art of the Italian Renaissance.[1] Evidently it appealed to other artists, working in a variety of media, and its wide diffusion suggests that other examples of the theme were also in existence, although this is the only antique version which is known today.

An equally curious interpretation of the piece is given by Benjamin of Tudela, who also saw it outside the Lateran when he visited the city of Rome in the year 1166. He identifies the boy as Absalom, son of the Old Testament king David, and Paul Borchardt has suggested that the upturned foot may have recalled to the rabbi's mind the words of 2 Samuel 14:25, "Now in all Israel there was no one so

---

[7.1] For the influence of the "Spinario" see in particular J. Adhémar, *Influences antiques dans l'art du moyen-âge français* (London 1939), pp. 189-192; W.S. Heckscher, "Dornauszieher," in *Reallexikon zur deutschen Kunstgeschichte* (Stuttgart 1958), 4: 289-299; D. Mouriki, "The Theme of the 'Spinario' in Byzantine Art," *Deltion tēs Christianikēs Archaiologikēs Heraireias* 6 (1970-1972), 53-66; R. Cocke, "Masaccio and the Spinario, Piero and the Pothos: Observations on the Reception of the Antique in Renaissance Painting," *Zeitschrift für Kunstgeschichte* 43 (1980), 21-32; F. Haskell and N. Penny, *Taste and the Antique* (New Haven 1981), pp. 308-310; and G. Fossi, "La représentation de l'Antiquité dans la sculpture romane et une figuration classique: le tireur d'épine," in *La Représentation de l'Antiquité au Moyen-Âge* (Vienne 1982), pp. 299-324.

much to be praised for his beauty as Absalom; from the sole of his foot to the crown of his head there was no blemish in him."²

8

Having described a number of individual bronze statues, Gregory now turns his attention to a large group of images known collectively as the "Salvatio civium." This legend concerning a series of statues representing the various tribes and peoples of the world, with bells which would ring if that nation took up arms against Rome, may be found with minor variations in a wide variety of medieval sources.¹ Its earliest recorded appearance is in the eighth century, in Cosmas of Jerusalem's commentary on Gregory of Nazianzus,² but its roots may go back considerably further, to the late years of the western empire.³ Rodocanachi suggests that it ultimately derives either from the great number of statues, representing various deities, which in antiquity were displayed in the Capitoline temples, or from Augustus's Porticus ad Nationes in the Campus Martius, which housed representations of the various gods of those countries subject to Rome.⁴ Whatever the initial inspiration, it was certainly well-known to medieval authors. The *Mirabilia* (cap. 16) also speaks of such a series of statues on the Capitoline,⁵ while one fifteenth-century German visitor to the city, Nicholas Muffel of Nuremburg, who made the journey south in order to attend the coronation of the Holy Roman Emperor

---

² P. Borchardt, "The Sculpture in Front of the Lateran as Described by Benjamin of Tudela and Magister Gregorius," *Journal of Roman Studies* 26 (1936), 68-70. For other interpretations see Gunter Schweikhart, "Von Priapus zu Coridon: Benennungen des Dornausziehers in Mittelalter und Neuzeit," *Würzburger Jahrbücher für die Altertumswissenschaft* 3 (1977), 243-252.

⁸·¹ See A. Graf, *Roma nella memoria e nelle immaginazioni del medio evo* (Turin 1915), pp. 148-161; E. Rodocanachi, *The Roman Capitol* (London 1906), pp. 58-63; and M. Demus-Quatember, "Zur Weltwunderliste des Pseudo-Beda und ihren Beziehungen zu Rom," *Römische Historische Mitteilungen* 12 (1970), 67-92.

² Cosmas Hierosolymitanus, *Commentarii in sancti Gregorii Nazianzeni carmina* (Migne, PG 38, col. 546).

³ Graf, p. 157.

⁴ Rodocanachi, pp. 60-61.

⁵ *Cod. topog.* 3: 34.

Frederick III in 1452, locates the images in the niches of the Pantheon.[6] The legend even circulated beyond the frontiers of Christendom: the Arab geographer Yaqut (d. 1229), in his description of Rome, speaks of one hundred statues holding bells, supposedly in the vicinity of the Lateran palace.[7] There is no doubt as to Gregory's own source of the information. He has taken his version of the tale from Pseudo-Bede's *De septem miraculis mundi*,[8] in which the "Salvatio civium" is the first of the seven *miracula* to be listed, and in the first part of the chapter Gregory repeats that text more or less verbatim. However, this version only carries the story to the point at which the priests carry the name of the statue to the city's governors, who then send an army to put down the rebellion. The balance of the chapter is either derived from other sources, or else from a more elaborate version of the *De septem miraculis mundi* which has not survived. The first addition, the bronze equestrian figure who aims his lance at the statue representing the rebellious nation, also appears in the version of the story told by the twelfth-century English scholar Alexander Neckam (1157-1217), in his *De naturis rerum*.[9] The second, that the hall collapsed and that its eternal fire was extinguished on the night that Christ was born, following a prediction that it would last "until a virgin gave birth," has no exact parallel although a number of similar tales are known to have been in circulation.[10] For example, the *Mirabilia* and the *Graphia aureae urbis* both cite this story in connection with a golden statue of Romulus, situated in a palace of the same name,[11] while

---

[6] A. Michaelis, "Le antichità della città di Roma descritte da Nicolao Muffel," *Mittheilungen des kaiserlich deutschen archaeologischen Instituts. Römische Abteilung* 3 (1888), 254-276, esp. 262. This may stem from a careless reading of the *Mirabilia*, which continues in the same chapter to describe the foundation of the Pantheon by Agrippa.

[7] See I. Guidi, "La descrizione di Roma nei geografi arabi," *Archivio della R. Società Romana di Storia Patria* 1 (1878), 173-218, esp. 184-185.

[8] For this text see the Introduction and the commentary to chapter six.

[9] Alexander Neckam, *De naturis rerum* 2, clxxiv: "Miles vero aeneus, equo insidens aeneo, in summitate fastigii praedicti palatii hastam vibrans, in illam se vertit partem quae regionem illam respiciebat."

[10] See Graf, pp. 253-256.

[11] *Cod. topog.* 3: 21, 82.

in a twelfth-century French version of the legend of St. Peter's chains, it is the "palace of Augustus" which collapses.[12]

Once again it is only Alexander Neckam's *De naturis rerum* which concurs with Gregory in associating this tale with the "Salvatio civium."[13] The close correspondence between these two works must surely be more than a mere coincidence, but it seems unlikely that Gregory has followed Neckam, or vice versa,[14] since in other respects their stories are very different. Neckam's statues are made of wood not bronze, are located in a "nobile palatium" constructed by the magician Virgil,[15] and there is no mention of any fire. Thus, although similar in some respects, the two also differ in fundamentals, and Neckam was clearly not using the *De septem miraculis mundi* as we know it. It seems more likely that, in addition to his principal source (i.e. the text erroneously attributed to Bede), Gregory also had access to another version or tradition of the story, and that he attempted to add a few details from the latter to complement the former. This second tradition, also used by Neckam, was clearly rather restricted in its circulation, providing further evidence to support the contention that Gregory was English.

It should be noted that at no point does Gregory state, or even imply, that he has actually seen this wonder. In fact, the impression he gives is precisely the reverse, and the statues are said to be among those works "which were once in Rome" ("que Rome quondam fuerunt"). He does, however, describe the ruins of a vaulted structure where, he believes, they formerly stood. The suggestion that the statues are no longer in Rome finds parallels in other versions of the

---

[12] "Eadem namque nocte qua Immaculata Virgo Maria Christum peperit, cecidit ipsum palacium." See J. van der Straeten, "Les chaînes de St. Pierre. Une nouvelle version de la légende," *Analecta Bollandiana* 90 (1972), 413-424.

[13] Alexander Neckam, *De naturis rerum* 2, clxxiv: "Quaesitus autem vates gloriosus quamdiu a diis conservandum esset illud nobile aedificium, respondere consuevit, 'Stabit usque dum pariat virgo'. Hoc autem audientes, philosopho applaudentes, dicebant, 'Igitur in aeternum stabit'. In nativitate autem Salvatoris, fertur dicta domus inclita subitam fecisse ruinam."

[14] Neckam's work was composed in the last quarter of the twelfth century, but as Gregory's dates are unknown, it is impossible to say which text is earlier.

[15] The idea that Virgil was a magician and necromancer seems to have been a popular one. It can also be found in the writings of Gervase of Tilbury and Vincent of Beauvais.

"Salvatio civium": for example the compiler of the tenth-century *Chronicon Salernitanum* states that they had been removed from Rome to Constantinople by the Byzantine emperor Alexander.[16]

9

The account of the iron statue of Bellerophon is again largely derived from Pseudo-Bede's *De septem miraculis mundi*, and again it is described in the past tense, with no suggestion that the author had actually seen it. Rushforth suggests that Gregory's manuscript copy of this list of world wonders may have read "in summa civitate" instead of "in Smyrna civitate," as one known copy does indeed do.[1]

A description of a statue at Alexandria, which remained suspended in mid air due to the equal forces exerted by an arc of magnets, is given by the Roman author Pliny, who attributes this feat of engineering to the architect Timochares.[2] The story is repeated in the fifth century by Augustine[3] and in the seventh by Isidore of Seville.[4] A statue of Bellerophon, showing him about to fly off on the winged horse Pegasus, located in the city of Smyrna, is mentioned in Cosmas of Jerusalem's eighth-century commentary on Gregory of Nazianzus,[5] and while it is not entirely clear how this developed into the magnetic "miracle" of the *De septem miraculis mundi*, Salomon Reinach has suggested that there is an easy transition from a statue which appears to have an insufficient base of support to one without any visible support whatsoever.[6] It is interesting to note that Alexander Neckam, in his discussion of magnetic stones, describes a statue of Mohammed

---

[16] See Nicola Cilento, "Sulla tradizione della 'Salvatio civium': la magica tutela della città medievale," in *Roma anno 1300*, ed. A.M. Romanini (Rome 1983), pp. 695-705.

[9-1] Rushforth, pp. 43-44.

[2] Pliny, *Natural History* 34.42.

[3] Augustine of Hippo, *De civitate Dei* 21.6.

[4] Isidore of Seville, *Etymologiae* 16, xxi, 4.

[5] Migne, PG 38, col. 547.

[6] S. Reinach, "Une statue de Bellérophon à Smyrne," *Revue Archéologique* 4 ser., 20 (1912), 330-333.

(location unspecified) which is similarly suspended in this fashion.[7] Pliny's tale clearly fascinated the medieval mind, and lived on in a variety of new versions.

10-11

The bath of "Apollo Bianeus" (a corruption of Apollonius of Tyana), which remained hot without any evident application of heat, is also described in the *De septem miraculis mundi*, where the corruption of the name of its maker had already taken place.[1] This source does not specify any particular location, and Gregory clearly associates it with a hot sulphurous bath which he visited somewhere in Rome, probably not far from the Lateran palace.[2] In this chapter we are given one of the personal glimpses which do so much to bring the *Narracio* alive. Although he had paid an entrance fee, the strong smell of the sulphur discouraged him from actually taking a bath, and he settles for putting his hand in, in order no doubt to test the temperature of the water.

Rushforth's proposal that a channel bringing such water from the thermal springs near Tivoli to Nero's Domus Aurea might still be functional some twelve centuries later seems implausible, but there is no obvious alternative.[3] No such bath is mentioned in any of the other medieval descriptions of the city.

The account of the theatre at Heraklea, with its perfect acoustics, is also taken from the *De septem miraculis mundi*. It is unclear whether Gregory believed this theatre to be in Rome, or whether he has included it because it appeared in his source. Indeed the digression from the subject of bronzes in these two chapters is difficult to

---

[7] Alexander Neckam, *De naturis rerum* 2.xcviii.

[10-1] The earliest extant manuscript of the *De septem miraculis mundi*, now in Munich (Bayerische Staatsbibliothek cod. lat. 22053), gives the name as "apolo do anius." See M. Demus-Quatember, "Zur Weltwunderliste des Pseudo-Beda und ihren Beziehungen zu Rom," *Römische Historische Mitteilungen* 12 (1970), 67-92, esp. 73.

[2] At the end of chapter 18 the location of the bath is specified with more precision as adjoining the aqueduct which passed the Lateran complex.

[3] Rushforth, pp. 33-34.

explain. Admittedly the story of the bath does feature a bronze vat, but there is no mention of any metal in the description of the theatre.

12

After a further reference to Pope Gregory I as a destroyer of pagan statuary (cf. chapter six), Gregory now begins a new section devoted to sculpture in marble. First to be described is a statue of Venus, which so captivated his attention that he returned three times to look at it. This reference is of particular interest since the Venus is not mentioned in other medieval sources. This is also one of those occasions in which some inkling of Gregory's own personality surfaces through the lines of the text, and he paints a vivid picture of this figure, which seems to him more like a living creature than a statue ("ut magis viva creatura videatur quam statua"). Since he knows Ovid, he may have in mind the story of Pygmalion, whose statue does come to life (*Metamorphoses* 10.243-297), although he does not quote from it directly. He does however include part of a line from Ovid's *Ars amatoria* (1.248), from the story of the Judgment of Paris. Rushforth has most plausibly suggested that perhaps this piece can be identified with the statue of Venus now in the Capitoline Museum, known as the "Capitoline Venus."[1] A clue to the geographical location is given at the end of the chapter when Gregory states that the statues of the Dioscuri, which have always stood on the Quirinal hill, are "non longe inde." In the reign of Pope Clement X (1667-1670) the Capitoline Venus was indeed found in this region, between the Quirinal and the Viminal hills in the gardens of the Stazi family opposite the church of San Vitale.[2] It was bought for the Capitoline collection by Benedict XIV in 1752, and may well be the figure which entranced Gregory with its magic. The marble is in fact Parian, and Gregory's observation of this is quite remarkable. In this instance he was apparently well-informed.

[12-1] Rushforth, p. 25.
[2] See Wolfgang Helbig, *Guide to the Public Collections of Classical Antiquities in Rome* (Leipzig 1895), 1: 338-339; and *A Catalogue of the Ancient Sculptures Preserved in the Municipal Collections of Rome. The Sculptures of the Museo Capitolino*, ed. H. Stuart Jones (Oxford 1912), pp. 182-184.

The two large horses are undoubtedly those of the Dioscuri on the Quirinal: the monumental statues of the twins Castor and Pollux. Their exact placement in antiquity is not known, but they were certainly in the region of the Quirinal,[3] and they are cited by the author of the Einsiedeln Itinerary (*circa* AD 800) in relation to the churches of S. Vitale and S. Susanna.[4] A number of buildings in this part of the city are identified in medieval texts by epithets such as "de caballis marmoreis," so they were evidently a prominent landmark.[5] After at least one restoration in the period of the Renaissance,[6] they were set up in their present fashion by Domenico Fontana in the time of Pope Sixtus V (1585-1590). The *Mirabilia* devotes an entire chapter to this group, narrating an elaborate story in which the statues are said to have been commissioned by the emperor Tiberius in order to honour two young philosophers named Phidias and Praxiteles.[7] These names derive from inscriptions carved on the bases of the statues (OPUS FIDIAE and OPUS PRAXITELIS), which the author of the *Mirabilia* (and presumably others in the twelfth century) did not recognize as being those of famous Greek sculptors of the fifth and fourth centuries BC respectively.[8] If Gregory knew this tale, he does not mention it. Instead he prefers to identify the two men as the "priorum compotistarum ymagines," interpreting the horses as symbolic of the quickness of their intellect. He does not give the source of this information, which again is unique to the *Narracio*.

---

[3] Probably in the Baths of Constantine. For the various identifications of the statues see F. Haskell and N. Penny, *Taste and the Antique* (New Haven 1981), pp. 136-141. For the dating and style of the group see Gerhart Egger, "Probleme konstantinischer Plastik," *Jahrbuch der Kunsthistorischen Sammlungen in Wien* 62 (1966), 71-102, esp. 72-76.

[4] *Cod. topog.* 2: 179, 184.

[5] Medieval and Renaissance references to the Dioscuri are examined by A. Michaelis, "Monte Cavallo," *Mittheilungen des kaiserlich deutschen archaeologischen Instituts. Römische Abtheilung* 13 (1898), 248-274.

[6] See Arnold Nesselrath, "Antico and Monte Cavallo," *The Burlington Magazine* 124 (1982), 353-357.

[7] *Mirabilia*, cap. 12 (*Cod. topog.* 3: 30-31).

[8] The earliest reference to the inscriptions occurs in the eleventh century (see Michaelis, "Monte Cavallo," p. 250), but presumably they go back to late antiquity when the names of the two sculptors were better known. The attributions are of course fanciful.

13

The reclining statues of Solomon and Bacchus can be identified as the statues of the river gods Nile and Tigris which today grace the front of the Palazzo Senatorio on the Capitoline hill.[1] Gregory is in complete accord with the *Mirabilia* (cap. 28) in placing them next to the Dioscuri, but the *Mirabilia* specifies the site more precisely as the "palace of Constantine" (i.e. the large baths which were constructed by this emperor on the Quirinal hill).[2] The decision to remove them to the Capitol was taken in the year 1517.[3]

The *Mirabilia* names the figures as the gods Saturn and Bacchus, as does the fourteenth-century humanist Giovanni Dondi in his *Iter Romanum*,[4] and Gregory's *Narracio* is the only source to refer to the first of the two as the Old Testament king Solomon. Rushforth suggests that this identification was possibly prompted by the object which he held, identified by our author as a sceptre.

14

This is the first of a number of buildings which Gregory refers to as a palace ("palatium"), although it is evident that by this term he means any large structure and not necessarily one which had been built specifically as a residence. From its proximity to the statues of the river gods and the Dioscuri, the site may be readily identified as the south-western corner of the Quirinal hill, and no "palaces" (in the modern sense of the term) are known to have been constructed in this area before the sixteenth century, at which time such activity

---

[1] E. Nash, *Pictorial Dictionary of Ancient Rome* (Tübingen 1962), 2: 442 and pls. 1248-1249. In the sixteenth century the "Tigris" was converted into a "Tiber" by replacing the tiger under the figure's arm with the Roman she-wolf and Romulus and Remus.

[2] *Cod. topog.* 3: 61. For their origin in the period *circa* AD 315-330 see Gerhart Egger, "Probleme konstantinischer Plastik," *Jahrbuch der Kunsthistorischen Sammlungen in Wien* 62 (1966), 71-102, esp. 71.

[3] The document ordering the transfer, dated 19 November 1517, is published by R. Lanciani, *Storia degli Scavi di Roma* (Rome 1902), 1: 182-183.

[4] *Cod. topog.* 4: 73.

became highly fashionable. The most imposing of these is the Quirinal Palace itself, begun in 1574, which has served in succession as a residence for the popes, the Italian royal family (1870-1947), and the president of the Italian Republic. In ancient times there were, however, two enormous structures in this immediate vicinity, both of which remained largely intact until the sixteenth century: the temple of Sarapis, constructed by the emperor Caracalla (AD 211-217) and the early-fourth-century Baths of Constantine.[1] I believe that Gregory has in mind the former of these two, although it is certainly possible that in their ruined state he did not distinguish between them.

The temple of Sarapis was a vast project which stood at the edge of the hill, on the site of the present villa Colonna, with its monumental staircase descending the slope to the area of what is now the Via della Pilotta. As it is known to have covered an area in excess of 13,000 m^2, with its columns more than 21 m. in height, it was bound to attract Gregory's attention, and it aptly fits his description as an "ampla ... et altissima domus". One single piece of the pediment,

---

[14-1] For the Baths of Constantine see Platner-Ashby, pp. 525-526; Maria Santangelo, "Il Quirinale nell' antichità classica," *Atti della Pontificia Accademia Romana di Archeologia. Memorie* 5 (1941), 77-214, esp. 203-208; and Ernest Nash, *Pictorial Dictionary of Ancient Rome* (Tübingen 1962), 2: 442. Its condition in the sixteenth century may be ascertained from the view by Du Pérac (published by Nash, pl. 1242). In the early seventeenth century the remnants were demolished to make way for the Palazzo Rospigliosi. Adjoining this structure was a large temple, the identification of which has been the subject of controversy. Numerous studies of the topography of ancient Rome since A. Fulvio's *Antiquitates urbis Romae* (1515) have thought it to be the Temple of the Sun built by the emperor Aurelian (270-275), and the arguments for this attribution are presented by R. Lanciani, "Di un frammento inedito della pianta di Roma antica riferibile alla Regione VII," *Bullettino della Commissione Archeologica Comunale di Roma* 22 (1894), 285-311, esp. 296-302, and M. Santangelo, pp. 154-177. The alternative view, that it is Caracalla's Sarapeum, is presented by C. Huelsen, "Il Tempio del Sole nella regione VII di Roma," *Bullettino della Commissione Archeologica Comunale di Roma* 23 (1895), 39-59. See also Platner-Ashby, pp. 491-492; Valentini-Zucchetti, *Cod. topog.* 1: 107 note 4; and Nash, *Pictorial Dictionary* 2: 376. This second view seems more probable in light of the evidence provided by the *Notitia urbis Romae regionum XIIII*. This fourth-century text places the Temple of Sarapis on the Quirinal (region VI), while the Temple of the Sun is listed in region VII (Via Lata), see *Cod. topog.* 1: 107, 111. Furthermore, part of an inscription mentioning the Sarapeum (*Corpus Inscriptionum Latinarum* 6.570), formerly set into the pavement of the church of S. Agata dei Goti, is said to have come from this area.

which still survives in the grounds of the villa Colonna, has been measured at 34.27 m³ and is estimated to weigh approximately 100 tons.² The temple was still standing in the Middle Ages, and its principal despoliation can be documented as having taken place in the sixteenth century, when its stone was cut for new use in buildings such as the Palazzo Farnese and the Villa Giulia.³

Gregory calls it the palace of the "Cornuti," or "horned men." This provides an additional clue to the geography, since a medieval church known as S. Salvatoris de Cornutis stood in this area until demolished by Pope Sixtus V in 1589.⁴ But how does the name originate? Both Rushforth and Valentini-Zucchetti accept the explanation provided to Gregory (who had presumably asked the same question himself): that the building bore this name because it had been the house of a Roman family with the cognomen Cornutus,⁵ and indeed a fragment of a Greek inscription mentioning a medical doctor by this name was seen in the fifteenth century.⁶ Rushforth then suggests that the horned images which Gregory saw may have been the carved decoration of ox heads (*bucrania*) on a family tomb or columbarium.

This solution seems unlikely for a variety of reasons, apart from the obvious objection that no Roman tomb would have stood on the Quirinal, within the perimeter of the Servian walls. Throughout the text of the *Narracio*, Gregory is clearly impressed by size, and in this passage he describes the height of the "palace" with the adjective "altissima." It seems unlikely that he can be referring to a private *domus* of modest proportions, and virtually inconceivable that he would do so when buildings the size of this temple, or the adjoining Baths of Constantine, stood in the same area. Furthermore, no family by this name is associated with the Quirinal in ancient sources.

---

² For these and other impressive measurements taken by antiquarians in the sixteenth century see Santangelo, p. 158.
³ *Ibid.*, pp. 160-161.
⁴ Christian Huelsen, *Le Chiese di Roma nel Medio Evo* (Florence 1927), pp. 435-436. The church is also mentioned in a papal bull of Celestine III (1191-1198), see P.F. Kehr, *Italia Pontificia* (Berlin 1906), 1: 62, and the fourteenth-century Turin catalogue lists it as having both "sacerdotum et clerum" (*Cod. topog.* 3: 292).
⁵ Rushforth, pp. 26-27, and Valentini-Zucchetti, *Cod. topog.* 3: 155 note 1.
⁶ See G.B. De Rossi in *Bullettino di Archeologia Cristiana* (1890), 87 note 2.

Gregory is frequently inaccurate when he proposes an explanation for a name or attribution, although he can scarcely be blamed for this since his own knowledge of Roman topography was at best precarious. He could only repeat what he had been told by others, and at least he had the sense to seek out the most informed opinion available. On the other hand, his physical descriptions of objects and buildings are vivid and personal, and they do not depend on information supplied by others. Thus if he states explicitly that he saw a group of statues, all of men with horns, there is no need to suppose that he was looking at *bucrania*. One of the statues, he says, is called Jupiter *arenosus*. This Jupiter "of the sands" is Jupiter or Zeus Ammon, and this epithet is undoubtedly derived from the Roman grammarian Servius who, in his commentary on Virgil's *Aeneid*, had identified the word "Ammon" as meaning "sand" (no doubt believing that it derived from the Greek word for sand, *ammos*).[7] Given the location of the great shrine of Zeus Ammon at the Siwah oasis in the Egyptian desert, this etymology must have appeared quite plausible. The same passage in Servius also provided its medieval readers with the information that the attributes of this god were a pair of ram's horns. Thus there is no reason to doubt Gregory's identification.

The existence of such a statue in Caracalla's Sarapeum is not only possible but indeed likely, since in the syncretistic world of Roman religion Jupiter Ammon was among the deities most closely associated with Sarapis.[8] The popularity of both cults in the Mediterranean world owed much to the person of Alexander the Great of Macedon who, following the advice of the oracle of Ammon at Siwah, founded the city of Alexandria in 331 BC with Sarapis as its patron deity.[9] The cult of Sarapis subsequently flourished under the Ptolemies, and the great Sarapeum in Alexandria survived until its destruction by fanatical Christians in AD 391. One of the other "cornuti" seen by Gregory may have been the cult statue of this god, since on occasion

---

[7] *Servii grammatici qui feruntur in Vergilii carmina commentarii*, ed. G. Thilo and H. Hagen (Leipzig 1923), 1: 498: commentary on the *Aeneid* 4. 196. The dependence on Servius was first noted by Rushforth, p. 27.

[8] See John Stambaugh, *Sarapis Under the Early Ptolemies* (Leiden 1972), p. 85.

[9] See C.B. Welles, "The Discovery of Sarapis and the Foundation of Alexandria," *Historia* 11 (1962), 271-298.

he too was depicted with the ram's horns of Ammon.[10] It is also possible that Sarapis's usual head ornament, a tapered basket known as a *kalathos*, was interpreted as a horn by medieval observers. Another statue may have depicted the Egyptian bull-god Apis, from whose cult that of Sarapis was derivative. Indeed, Gregory's statement does much to confirm the identification of the temple on the Quirinal slope as Caracalla's Sarapeum.

15

The "palace" of Diocletian, which again impresses Gregory by its size, is presumably the largest bath complex in Rome, located on the Quirinal hill, and associated with the emperor Diocletian although actually constructed by his imperial colleague Maximian between AD 298 and 305/306.[1] The appellation may well have derived from the dedication inscription, intact at least as late as the Carolingian era when it was copied by the compiler of the Einsiedeln Itinerary, in which Diocletian's name was given first.[2] Large parts of this building still remain, and in the years 1563-1566 the central hall was converted into the church of S. Maria degli Angeli by Michelangelo. It is possible that Gregory did not know the original function of the structure, although in the *Mirabilia* it is included in the chapter on baths and not in the list of palaces.[3] However, in the late Middle Ages the word "palace" does seem to have been used as a generic term for any large structure, regardless of its function. Another twelfth-century author, Abbot Suger of St. Denis (1081-1151), who not only knew this building but who even made plans to ship some of its enormous columns to France for the reconstruction of his abbey near

---

[10] Stambaugh, p. 85.

[15-1] For the Baths of Diocletian see Platner-Ashby, pp. 527-530; Maria Santangelo, "Il Quirinale nell' antichità classica," *Atti della Pontificia Accademia Romana di Archeologia. Memorie* 5 (1941), 77-214, esp. 192-203; and E. Nash, *Pictorial Dictionary of Ancient Rome* (Tübingen 1962), 2: 448.

[2] *Corpus Inscriptionum Latinarum* 6: 1130. For the Einsiedeln Itinerary see *Cod. topog.* 2: 164.

[3] *Mirabilia*, cap. 5 (*Cod. topog.* 3: 20).

Paris, also calls it a "palace" of Diocletian, although clearly aware that it was a bath.[4]

Again the reader is given a personal glimpse: we are told that the columns are so high that no one is able to throw a stone to the top. One can easily imagine that Gregory had attempted to do so himself.

16

The identification of the Temple of Pallas, the only "templum" mentioned by Gregory apart from the Pantheon (ch. 21), presents a problem since he does not provide any information concerning its whereabouts. The *Mirabilia* refers to no less than three temples by this title: one in the Forum (possibly to be identified with the Temple of Castor and Pollux),[1] one on the Palatine,[2] and a third on the Aventine.[3] However, Rushforth and Valentini-Zucchetti have rejected all of these possibilities in favour of the Temple of Minerva in the Forum of Nerva, a structure which remained largely intact until the year 1606, when it was demolished by Pope Paul V to provide marble for the fountain of the Aqua Paola on the Janiculum.[4] Rushforth was led to this identification by Gregory's reference to the site as being a place where early Christians suffered torture and martyrdom if they refused to worship the image of Pallas. His reasoning is apparently as follows: a number of martyrologies refer to the location of the city prefecture, the place where sentences were passed, as being "in Tellude ante templum Palladis," and the actual site of the prefecture has been established by the discovery of inscriptions as being not far away from the Forum of Nerva in the vicinity of the church of

---

[4] Erwin Panofsky, *Abbot Suger on the Abbey Church of St. Denis and its Art Treasures*, 2nd ed., (Princeton 1979), pp. 90-91.

[16-1] *Cod. topog.* 3: 56. This identification is proposed by L. Duchesne, "Notes sur la topographie de Rome au moyen âge," *Mélanges d'Archéologie et d'Histoire* 9 (1889), 346-362, esp. 352.
[2] *Cod. topog.* 3: 57.
[3] *Ibid.*, p. 61.
[4] Ernest Nash, *Pictorial Dictionary of Ancient Rome* (Tübingen 1961), 1: 433.

S. Pietro in Vincoli.[5] Rushforth then suggests that the "horreum cardinalium" was related to the nearby Tor de' Conti, a fortified tower the base of which still stands, constructed in 1203 by the brother of the Conti pope, Innocent III (1198-1216).[6] Since a number of the cardinals at this time were members of the Conti family, a warehouse adjoining their stronghold might have been known popularly by such a title. If so, the early years of the thirteenth century would constitute a *terminus post quem* for Gregory's visit.

This identification of the "templum Palladis" is not, however, totally convincing. Although not a great distance away, the prefecture could scarcely be described as "ante" the Forum of Nerva, and Hippolyte Delehaye has issued a warning against putting any faith in the validity of textual references to the entire phrase "in Tellude ante templum Palladis."[7] In any case, the important point is not the location of the temple of Pallas/Minerva near the prefecture, but rather the location of a temple which was identified by this title in the Middle Ages, when the site of the prefecture is not likely to have been known. The temple in the Forum of Nerva was known to the author of the *Mirabilia* as the temple of the deified Nerva,[8] not as that of Pallas. Nor is there any link between this site and the name of Pallas in any other medieval texts. As has been noted, however, there were some three temples in the city which the *Mirabilia* does specifically link with Pallas, and it is undoubtedly to one of these that Gregory refers. We should also, then, probably look elsewhere

---

[5] See R. Lanciani, "Gli edifici della prefettura urbana fra la Tellure e le terme di Tito e di Traiano," *Bullettino della Commissione Archeologica Comunale di Roma* 20 (1892), 19-37; and Platner-Ashby, p. 432.

[6] Rushforth, pp. 30-31. For the history of the tower see Emma Amadei, *Le Torri di Roma* 3rd ed. (Rome 1969), pp. 20-24.

[7] H. Delehaye, "L'amphithéâtre Flavien et ses environs dans les textes hagiographiques," *Analecta Bollandiana* 16 (1897), 209-252, esp. 235: "On voudrait pouvoir expliquer l'expression 'in Tellude ante templum Palladis.' Le temple de Minerve ou de Pallas, du forum du Nerva ou *forum transitorium* ... n'était pas fort éloigné de la préfecture urbaine. Mais il est impossible d'admettre que l'aire qui recevait son nom du temple de Tellus embrassât le forum de Nerva. La formule citée est donc absolument vide de sens au point de vue topographique."

[8] *Cod. topog.* 3: 54. This appellation likely derives either from the name of the emperor which began the dedication inscription or else through general confusion of the names Nerva and Minerva.

for the "horreum cardinalium." If the "templum Palladis" is the one on the Palatine, the granary could have been part of the large Frangipane fortress, the "turris cartularia," in which Pope Innocent II had sought refuge in AD 1130, along with those cardinals who supported him. However, from the scanty information which Gregory supplies, no positive identification seems possible.

The reference to the *passio* of Hippolytus is interesting, if for no other reason than the fact that it is the only such Christian intrusion in the whole of the *Narracio*. The Hippolytus in question is clearly the one associated with the Roman deacon Lawrence, who suffered martyrdom in the reign of the emperor Decius (AD 249-251) by being tied to wild horses and torn apart.[9] The account of his passion, which also describes the deaths of others in his family, was evidently known to Gregory. It should be noted, however, that the text does not specify any particular site, nor does it mention a statue of Pallas.

17

Both Rushforth and Valentini-Zucchetti concur that the structure which Gregory probably has in mind is the Domus Augustana on the Palatine. This has no connection with the emperor Augustus, but was the imperial residence ("house of the augustus") from the time of the emperor Domitian (AD 81-96) onwards.[1] Despite some difficulties in this interpretation, not the least of which is the fact that the main palace on the Palatine is apparently referred to again by a different title in chapter 20, there do not appear to be any viable alternatives, and it accords well with the information provided at the beginning of the next chapter to the effect that the aqueduct of the Aqua Claudia was close by. There can be no doubt that Gregory has Augustus in mind, since he refers to the emperor's modesty in always shunning

---

[9] The text is edited by H. Delahaye, "Recherches sur le légendier romain," *Analecta Bollandiana* 51 (1933), 34-98, esp. 95: "Beati vero Yppoliti pedes iussit ligari ad colla equorum indomitorum et sic per cardetum et tribulos trahi; qui dum traheretur emisit spiritum." There can be little doubt that the story ultimately derives from the classical Hippolytus, son of Theseus, who also meets his death in this fashion.

[17-1] Cf. Platner-Ashby, pp. 158-166. Ashby (p. 159 note 1) disagrees with this view, however, preferring to place Gregory's palace closer to the Lateran.

the title "dominus." This story is told by Suetonius (Augustus liii), and repeated almost word for word by Orosius in the fifth century (*Historiae adversum paganos* 6.22) and Isidore of Seville in the seventh century (*Etymologiae* 9.iii.17), so Gregory could have obtained it from a number of possible sources. It was certainly known in late medieval Rome, since a similar statement about Augustus appears in the *Graphia aureae urbis* (cap. 22),[2] although not in the original version of the *Mirabilia*.

Nothing is known of any throne with an inscription such as that which Gregory describes, but if he did see a piece of a throne (and why should he invent this?), then clearly some sort of imperial residence is meant, and not a bath or some other large structure masquerading as a "palatium." Rushforth notes that the adjective "clementissimus" (here translated as "most merciful") does not appear in imperial inscriptions before the mid third century, when it may be found in Rome for the first time on the Arch of Gallienus (AD 262),[3] but there is no reason why the throne, or at least the inscription, could not date from the period of the late empire.

Gregory states without further comment that the site had provided quantities of material for the building of churches in the city, and indeed there are few medieval churches in Rome which were not constructed on, in or of classical materials. This was particularly true of the boom in church construction which had taken place in the first half of the twelfth century, which is to say not long before Gregory's visit.[4]

18

The aqueduct, which is later mentioned as entering the city at the

---

[2] *Cod. topog.* 3: 90.

[3] *Corpus Inscriptionum Latinarum* 6: 1 (Berlin 1876), no. 1106.

[4] The subject is eloquently examined by Richard Krautheimer, *Rome: Profile of a City, 312-1308* (Princeton 1980), pp. 161-202. For a more general treatment of the medieval re-use of the spoils of classical antiquity see A. Esch, "Spolien," *Archiv für Kulturgeschichte* 51 (1969), 1-64. The destruction of the remains of the ancient city was already being lamented some eight hundred years earlier, see Cassiodorus *Variae* 7.xiii (Migne, PL 69, col. 717).

Porta Asinaria, is undoubtedly that of the Neronian branch of the Aqua Claudia, although it does not in fact enter at this gate, but further to the east by the Porta Maggiore, from which point it passes to the north of the Lateran basilica on its route to the Caelian and Palatine hills. The Aqua Claudia, which has its source in the Aniene valley near Subiaco, was begun by the emperor Caligula in AD 38, but only completed under his successor Claudius, from whom it takes its name. It was dedicated in AD 52. The extension to the Caelian was constructed by Nero, and the further extension across the valley to the Palatine was undertaken by Domitian.[1] The metal pipes, which were of lead not copper, are described in the principal source of information concerning the water supply of ancient Rome: a book entitled *De aquae ductu*, written by Sextus Iulius Frontinus, who held the post of *curator aquarum* at the end of the first century AD.[2]

In the Middle Ages the gradual decay of the aqueduct system led to the concentration of the population of Rome along the banks of the Tiber river, which became the principal source of water supply. The aqueducts were not completely forgotten, however, and in the eighth century no less than four were repaired and restored to use by Pope Hadrian I (772-795).[3] These included the Aqua Claudia, which was of major importance since it supplied the papal palace at the Lateran, and as a result it is sometimes referred to in medieval sources as the *forma Lateranense*.[4] This system was probably still in operation at the time of Gregory's visit, since further repairs and modifications had been undertaken in the early twelfth century by Pope Honorius II (1124-1130). His biographer records that "he diverted water from ancient channels and brought it to the Lateran gate," creating a small lake which provided irrigation for vineyards and

---

[18.1] For a complete account of this aqueduct see Thomas Ashby, *The Aqueducts of Ancient Rome* (Oxford 1935), pp. 190-251. See also Harry Evans, "Nero's 'Arcus Caelimonti'," *American Journal of Archaeology* 87 (1983), 392-399.

[2] The text and photographs of the only known manuscript copy are published by Clemens Herschel, *The Water Supply of the City of Rome* (Boston 1899).

[3] These were the Claudia, the Jovia, the Virgo and the Sabbatina (see *Liber Pontificalis* 1: 503-505).

[4] The Einsiedeln Itinerary, for example, refers to it both as the "forma Claudiana" and the "forma Lateranense" (see *Cod. topog.* 2: 196, 198).

fruit trees.[5] If this activity involved the actual construction of a new conduit, and not simply the tapping of the Aqua Claudia, then Gregory may be correct in referring to the Porta Asinaria (the "Lateran gate" of Honorius II's biography) and not to the Porta Maggiore.[6] The statement that the Tiber water was unfit for human consumption probably reflected the opinion of most northern visitors to Rome, who even today prefer to drink *acqua minerale* and not that which comes from a tap. This is perhaps something of an overstatement on Gregory's part, since although the Tiber water was much less healthy than that supplied by the aqueducts, and more easily contaminated, it must certainly have been used by the medieval population of the city who had few other sources of supply.

He again mentions the bath of Apollo Bianeus, which had been the subject of chapter ten, adding the information that it was located beside the aqueduct.

19

This chapter comprises little more than a list of two "houses" and four "palaces," none of which can be identified with certainty. As the houses of Aquila and Fronto are supposedly located near the bath of Apollo Bianeus, Rushforth sets them on the Esquiline hill, and proposes that the "domus Aquileia" is either a corruption of "domus Esquilina" or else that it comes from the "domus Aquilii Iureconsulti."[1] The latter, however, is not well attested.[2] Another possibility is that Gregory is alluding to the house of Aquila and Priscilla, early converts to Christianity who appear in the New Testament Book of Acts and

---

[5] *Liber Pontificalis* 2: 379: "Hic etiam derivavit aquam de antiquis formis et ad portam Lateranensem conduxit, ibique lacum pro adaquandis equis fieri fecit; plurima quoque molendina in eadem aqua construxit, et multas vineas cum fructiferis arboribus secus ipsum lacum plantari studiosissime fecit."

[6] Rushforth, p. 34, prefers to translate Gregory's phrase "aque ductus qui per portam Assinariam descendit" as "the aqueduct which comes down *past* the porta Asinaria" (my italics), in which case there is no difficulty. This use of the preposition "per" is certainly possible in the Middle Ages.

[19-1] Rushforth, pp. 34-35.

[2] It appears in a late version of the *Notitia urbis Romae regionum XIIII* (*Cod. topog.* 1: 215).

a number of the Pauline epistles. Their house in Rome was later identified with the church of S. Prisca on the Aventine.[3] This would be most uncharacteristic, however, as his interest in monuments with Christian associations is distinctly conspicuous by its absence. Marcus Cornelius Fronto was a writer and orator of the second century AD who is thought to have been the teacher of the emperors Marcus Aurelius and Lucius Verus. Apparently he did possess property on the Esquiline, in an area which had once formed part of the gardens of Maecenas. This is known both from a reference to the gardens in one of his letters to Marcus Aurelius[4] and from direct archaeological evidence.[5] However, as neither name appears in the *Mirabilia* or any of the other guides, it is virtually impossible to determine Gregory's intention.[6]

All four "palaces" are associated with the names of early emperors: Tiberius, Nero, Nerva and Octavian. In its list of buildings on the Esquiline hill, the *Mirabilia* includes a "temple of the gods in the palace of Tiberius,"[7] but this has not yet been identified with any known structure. In the light of Gregory's possible interest in the Roman martyr Hippolytus (cf. ch. 16), it is perhaps worth noting that a palace of Tiberius is twice mentioned in the *Passio SS. Sixti, Laurentii et Hippolyti* as an imperial hall still in use in the time of the third-century emperor Decius.[8] There is also a "domus Tiberiana" on the Palatine.

The palace of Nero was usually identified in medieval sources with the Vatican circus, which had been completed in the time of Nero.[9] There are however two exceptions. In the Einsiedeln Itinerary

---

[3] Rushforth, p. 35 note 3.

[4] *The Correspondence of Marcus Cornelius Fronto*, ed. C.R. Haines (London 1955), 1: 122.

[5] Fronto's name appears on a water pipe found at this site in 1875, see *Notizie degli Scavi* 3 (1877), 85. The inscription is published in the *Corpus Inscriptionum Latinarum* (Berlin 1899), vol. 15, no. 7438.

[6] There is also a house of Fronto, evidently a wealthy patron of the arts, mentioned by Juvenal (*Saturae* 1. 12). Cf. Rushforth, p. 35, and Platner-Ashby, p. 181.

[7] *Mirabilia*, cap. 28: "In palatio Tiberii templum deorum" (*Cod. topog.* 3: 61).

[8] See H. Delehaye, "Recherches sur le légendier romain," *Analecta Bollandiana* 51 (1933), 89, 93.

[9] For this identification see *Liber Pontificalis* 1: 118, 150, and *Cod. topog.* 3: 22, 82, 85, 184, 396.

a "palatius Neronis" is listed after the church of Saints Cosmas and Damian in the Forum,[10] and the *Graphia aureae urbis* twice refers to the Lateran palace by this alternative name,[11] presumably recalling that Nero had confiscated this property from Plautius Lateranus in the aftermath of the Piso conspiracy.

No other source mentions a palace of Nerva, although the *Mirabilia* does speak of a palace which comprises in part the forum of this emperor and its temple,[12] and this may be the structure to which Gregory refers.

One cannot help but wonder what distinction there was in Gregory's mind between Octavian and Augustus, and whether the palace of the former (cited in this chapter) was considered different from that of the latter (already discussed in chapter 17). Presumably it was, and on the basis of the assumption that the Palatine is not here intended, we must look elsewhere. There are a number of possibilities. The *Mirabilia* includes a "palatium Octaviani" in its list of palaces (cap. 6), which both Rushforth and Valentini-Zucchetti link with the Capitoline in light of the popular legends concerning Augustus and the *ara caeli*.[13] The compiler or scribe responsible for Nicolas Rosell's fourteenth-century edition of the *Mirabilia* thought otherwise however, and to the entry added the phrase "ad sanctum Laurentium in Lucina,"[14] probably thinking of the Mausoleum of Augustus which is situated not far from this church. The earlier edition of the *Mirabilia* also

---

[10] *Cod. topog.* 2: 195. This has been provisionally identified as the Basilica of Constantine by Lanciani, "L'Itinerario di Einsiedeln e l'Ordine di Benedetto Canonico," *Monumenti Antichi* 1 (1890-1892), 438-551, esp. 494.

[11] *Cod. topog.* 3: 81, 91.

[12] *Mirabilia*, cap. 24: "Infra hunc terminum fuit palatium cum duobus foris: Nervae cum templo suo divi Nervae ..." (*Cod. topog.* 3: 54).

[13] Rushforth, p. 36; *Cod. topog.* 3: 158 note 4. The *Mirabilia* makes this link explicit in two separate passages: "Haec visio fuit in camero Octaviani imperatoris, ubi nunc est ecclesia Sanctae Mariae in Capitolio. Idcirco dicta est Sancta Maria Ara Caeli." (*Cod. topog.* 3: 29), and "In loco ubi nunc est Sancta Maria, fuere duo templa simul cum palatio ... ubi Octavianus imperator vidit visionem in caelo." (*ibid.*, 3: 52). The early-fifteenth-century *Tractatus de rebus antiquis et situ urbis Romae*, following in the same tradition, gives: "Palatium Octaviani fuit ubi nunc Sancta Maria Ara Caeli" (*Cod. topog.* 4: 127).

[14] *Cod. topog.* 3: 184.

refers to the mausoleum in another passage, calling it the "castellum" of Octavian.[15] Either site is possible.

At the end of the chapter we are finally on firmer ground with the "Septem Solia," about which Gregory says that he will keep silent. This is a common medieval name for the Septizonium,[16] the large structure located at the south-east corner of the Palatine hill, on the site of the present Piazza di Porta Capena. It was built by the emperor Septimius Severus after his return to Rome in AD 203. There is some apparent uncertainty on Gregory's part about the couplet quoted from Ovid's *Metamorphoses* (2.1-2), although it is slightly ambiguous whether the uncertainty concerns the attribution of the lines to Ovid or their application to this monument. The latter appears to be more likely, and if so Gregory has good reason to be dubious, since Ovid lived some two centuries before the Septizonium was constructed. However, as it was believed to be a temple of the Sun,[17] and as it did indeed stand high on "lofty columns," the error is easily explained.

20

Gregory's implication that this is a palace of enormous size has led Rushforth to identify it with the "palatium maius in Pallanteo" of the *Mirabilia*,[1] in other words the principal imperial residence which occupied the southern half of the Palatine hill, constructed for the most part by the emperor Domitian (AD 81-96). It is not certain how this is to be considered different from the palace of Augustus (ch. 17), assuming that the identification of that structure with the "Domus Augustana" was correct, but that Gregory here intends to refer to the principal palace is also suggested by his claim that it was the

---

[15] *Mirabilia*, cap. 22: "Ad portam Flammineam fecit Octavianus quoddam castellum quod voctaur Augustum, ubi sepelirentur imperatores, quod tabulatum fuit diversis lapidibus." (*Cod. topog.* 3: 47).

[16] Cf. *Cod. topog.* 3: 22, 24, 39, 187, 189. For the history of the structure see Platner-Ashby, pp. 473-475, and C. Huelsen, *Das Septizonium des Septimius Severus* (Berlin 1886).

[17] *Mirabilia*, cap. 25 (*Cod. topog.* 3: 58).

[20-1] *Cod. topog.* 3: 21.

residence of sixty emperors. Given the inaccuracy of his numbers in other contexts, one should be wary of according too much significance to this figure. Rushforth noted that Giraldus Cambrensis, in his *De principis instructione*, spoke of Tiberius II (578-582) as the fiftieth Roman emperor, that on this basis the sixtieth would be Theodosius III (715-717), and that "as it was the iconoclastic policy of his successor, Leo the Isaurian, which brought about the revolt of Rome and Byzantine Italy in 728, Theodosius was practically the last Eastern emperor to be recognized without question in Rome. At any rate, a later age may well have thought so."[2] This is an ingenious but unlikely theory, since the Italian opposition was not to the emperor *per se* but rather to his religious policy, and the Roman chancellery and mint would continue to use the imperial name for documents and coins for another generation.[3] In any case, this particular reckoning of the number of emperors was not the only one, nor indeed the only one to be known in England. Bede begins a chapter of his *Ecclesiastical History* (1.xxiii) with the remark that in AD 582 the emperor Maurice, "the fifty-fourth from Augustus," ascended the throne and ruled for twenty-one years.[4] By this count, the sixtieth would be Justinian II (685-695, 705-711).

However, it is more likely that the number was arbitrary, or at best approximate, and there are at least two other twelfth-century references in a similar vein. The first appears in the account of Benjamin of Tudela, visitor to Rome about the year 1166, who describes the ruined palaces in these words: "And around the part of Rome wherein men dwell, are spread out twenty and four miles of ruins. And there be found therein eighty palaces of eighty full mighty kings, that all be called emperors from Tarquin's reign unto the reign of Pepin son of Charles, who first conquered Spain."[5]

---

[2] Rushforth, p. 36.

[3] See discussion by Philip Grierson, *Catalogue of the Byzantine Coins in the Dumbarton Oaks Collection* (Washington 1973), 3: 89-91.

[4] *Bede's Ecclesiastical History of the English People*, ed. B. Colgrave and R.A.B. Mynors (Oxford 1969), p. 69. The precise count varies marginally from author to author: for example, Cassiodorus, writing in the early sixth century, lists forty-eight emperors ending with Anastasius, (Migne, PL 69, cols. 1226-1248). Continuing this count would make Maurice the fifty-third.

[5] Francis Nichols, *The Marvels of Rome* (London 1889), pp. 53-54.

Bridging the gap between Benjamin's eighty and Gregory's sixty, and with specific reference to the large palace on the Palatine hill, is a notice in a twelfth-century manuscript of the *Descriptio Lateranensis ecclesiae* which lists the monastery of San Cesario as being "in palatio LXX regum."[6] Thus there is some outside evidence for referring to the palace as having been the residence of a large number of rulers, as indeed was the case. The last of the emperors to actually do so was Constans II, who visited Rome briefly in the year 663,[7] and the palace ceased to be maintained only in the middle of the eighth century.[8]

21

The Pantheon in its present form was constructed during the early years of the reign of the emperor Hadrian (AD 117-138) on the site of an earlier structure which had been completed by Marcus Agrippa in 25 BC.[1] Agrippa's name is preserved in the principal inscription on the facade. It was perhaps the first of the city's pagan temples to be re-dedicated to Christian use, this being accomplished by Pope Boniface IV in AD 609,[2] and Gregory's reference to the building as the "idolium omnium deorum, immo demonum" seems to echo the *Mirabilia*'s comment that, prior to its conversion to a church, Christians

---

[6] Biblioteca Apostolica Vaticana, cod. Reg. lat. 712, fol. 89. See *Cod. topog.* 3: 361 or C. Huelsen, *Le Chiese di Roma nel Medio Evo* (Florence 1927), p. 128. The site has been identified by A. Bartoli, "Scoperta dell' oratorio e del monastero di S. Cesario sul Palatino," *Nuovo Bullettino di Archeologia Cristiana* 13 (1907), 191-204.

[7] The visit is described in detail in the *Liber Pontificalis* 1: 343-344. For the subsequent medieval history of the Palatine see G. Carettoni, "Il Palatino nel Medioevo," *Studi Romani* 9 (1961), 508-518.

[8] See Paolo Verzone, "La distruzione dei palazzi imperiali di Roma e di Ravenna e la ristrutturazione del palazzo Lateranense nel IX secolo nei rapporti con quello di Costantinopoli," *Roma e l'Età Carolingia* (Rome 1976), 39-54.

[21-1] The literature on the Pantheon is enormous, but recent studies in English include Kjeld Licht, *The Rotunda in Rome* (Copenhagen 1968) and William MacDonald, *The Pantheon* (London 1976).

[2] The event and the new dedication are recorded in the *Liber Pontificalis* 1: 317.

passing by were tormented by demons.³ The dedication of the altar to Mary combined with the shape of the structure to produce its medieval name which Gregory records: S. Maria Rotunda. He is also aware of the additional dedication to "all saints." The *Mirabilia*, which devotes a lengthy chapter to the Pantheon and to its seventh-century conversion, does not however actually describe the building, and thus Gregory is the earliest known witness to the statuary placed before the entrance portico.

The lions are presumably those carved of grey granite which were set on pedestals in front of the temple in the reign of Pope Clement VII (1523-1534).⁴ They are shown in this fashion in a drawing made later in the sixteenth century by Martin van Heemskerck, now in the Kupferstichkabinett, Berlin.⁵ One lion had been "discovered" in the fifteenth century, in the time of Pope Eugenius IV (1431-1447) who had cleared the square of much of its accumulated earth and debris. The second had come to light during Clement VII's reign. In 1586 they were both removed by order of Pope Sixtus V in order to grace the fountain at the termination of the Acqua Felice (at the corner of the present Via Orlando and Via Venti Settembre). Here they were put to use as water spouts, until moved again by Gregory XVI (1831-1846), who placed them in the new Egyptian Museum which he had founded in the Vatican Palace. They remain in the Vatican today, and those on the fountain are copies. Both lions bear the name of the last of the Egyptian pharoahs, Nektanebo II (30th dynasty), who lost his kingdom to the Persians in the middle of the fourth century BC, shortly before they lost it in turn to Alexander of Macedon. If, as seems likely, they stood before the Pantheon in antiquity, then they may well have been brought to Rome during the reign of Augustus, along with other spoils from the Egyptian campaign.⁶ They would

---

³ *Mirabilia*, cap. 16 (*Cod. topog.* 3: 34-35). This view was a common one, see T. Buddensieg, "Criticism and Praise of the Pantheon in the Middle Ages and the Renaissance," in *Classical Influences on European Culture, A.D. 500-1500*, ed. R. Bolgar (Cambridge 1971), pp. 259-267.

⁴ For the history of the lions see Orazio Marucchi, "I leoni del re Nektanebo," *Bullettino della Commissione Archeologica Comunale di Roma* 18 (1890), 307-325; and Anne Roullet, *The Egyptian and Egyptianizing Monuments of Imperial Rome* (Leiden 1972), pp. 131-132, cat. nos. 273, 274.

⁵ Reproduced by Licht, fig. 14.

⁶ Marucchi, pp. 322-324.

thus have been available to Agrippa in 27-25 BC when the first Pantheon was constructed. The alternative theory, that they were among the decorations of the nearby Iseum Campense,[7] seems less likely in the light of Gregory's evidence.

A porphyry "concha," quite possibly the one which Gregory mentions, was found with the first lion in the time of Eugenius IV, and it remained in front of the Pantheon into the eighteenth century.[8] It appears prominently in the square, about half way between the portico and the fountain, in the mid-seventeenth-century engraving by G.B. Falda.[9] It now serves as the tomb of pope Clement XII (d. 1740) in the Corsini chapel in S. Giovanni in Laterano.

The figure for the width of the building, which our author claims to have measured himself, is given as 266 "pedes." The fact that Gregory would make such a measurement seems entirely in keeping with his curious nature,[10] but the number itself is puzzling since the actual width of the interior is 43.80 m. or 148 Roman feet (1 Roman foot = approx. 29.5 cm.).[11] Of course we have no way of knowing whether this measurement includes the portico (which would add another 15.50 m.), or indeed what sort of "foot" Gregory was using. It seems most likely that the *pes* in question would have been his own, and perhaps, as Richard Krautheimer has recently suggested, he simply had small feet![12]

The chapter concludes with a bitter complaint against the cupidity of the Roman people, whom Gregory blames for having stripped the roof of the Pantheon of its gilded bronze tiles. The charge is accurate, although aimed at the wrong party. This act was committed not by the people of Rome but rather by the emperor Constans II, during

---

[7] Roullet, p. 131.

[8] Marucchi, p. 323. However, Platner-Ashby, p. 385, suggest that it came from the nearby Baths of Agrippa.

[9] *Il Nuovo Teatro delle Fabbriche, et Edifici, in prospettiva di Roma Moderna*, ed. G. Rossi (Rome 1665), fol. 31.

[10] Pantheon measurements are also included in Giovanni Dondi's *Iter Romanum*, written *circa* 1375 (see *Cod. topog.* 4: 69).

[11] Licht, p. 195.

[12] Richard Krautheimer, *Rome: Profile of a City, 312-1308* (Princeton 1980), p. 189.

COMMENTARY, CH. 22   79

his brief visit to the city in the summer of the year 663.[13] Nor would this be the last such act of vandalism that the Pantheon would suffer. Four centuries after Gregory's lament, Pope Urban VIII (1623-1644) of the Barberini family would remove the bronze roof trusses of the portico. The metal was used to cast eighty cannon for the Castel Sant' Angelo, and the deed prompted the famous pasquinade "Quod non fecerunt barbari, fecerunt Barberini" (What the barbarians haven't accomplished, the Barberini have).[14] The quotation from Virgil's *Aeneid* (3.57), "auri sacra fames," was widely used in the Middle Ages in this sort of context,[15] and Gregory's complaint about the stripping of metal from temples curiously echoes one made some seven centuries earlier by the Ostrogothic king, Theodoric, in a letter to the Roman Senate.[16]

22

This is the first of three arches which are described by Gregory in some detail, none of which can be easily identified with the three principal triumphal arches which still stand in Rome today: those of Titus (AD 81), Septimius Severus (AD 203) and Constantine (AD 315). The arch in question, we are informed, is "multiplex" (presumably then a triple arch), dedicated to Augustus, and decorated with numerous statues and reliefs depicting the victories of the emperor. He identifies in particular the Battle of Actium (31 BC), the flight of Cleopatra, and her subsequent suicide.

Augustus is known to have been honoured by two triumphal arches. The first, located in the Forum according to Dio Cassius, and known from coins to have consisted of a single arch, was erected by Senatorial decree soon after the Battle of Actium. The second, a triple arch, was built in 19 BC to record the recovery of the Roman standards from the Parthians. The foundations of the latter were excavated and

---

[13] *Liber Pontificalis* 1: 343, and Paulus Diaconus, *Historia Langobardorum* 5, 11. See also Frank Moore, "The Gilt-Bronze Tiles of the Pantheon," *American Journal of Archaeology* 3 (1899), 40-43.

[14] See Licht, p. 241.

[15] For example Gregory of Tours, *History of the Franks* 4. 46; Liutprand of Cremona, *Antapodosis* 1. xxxii.

[16] See C. Davis-Weyer, *Early Medieval Art, 300-1150. Sources and Documents* (Englewood Cliffs, N.J., 1971), pp. 51-52.

identified by Otto Richter in 1888, in the Forum on the southern edge of the Temple of Julius Caesar. More recently the base of the earlier arch has also come to light in the same vicinity, on the east side of the triple arch. Thus it would appear that the single arch built to commemorate the victory at Actium was demolished in 19 BC to make way for the second, and larger, memorial.[1] There is, however, no archaeological evidence which suggests that the triple arch was adorned with narrative relief panels, or that it was still standing in the Middle Ages. Moreover, Gregory locates his arch near the Pantheon, a long way from the Forum. One can only conclude that either Gregory was mistaken in his identification, or else that there existed yet another Arch of Augustus which is not otherwise recorded in ancient sources.

The *Mirabilia* (cap. 3) provides a lengthy list of the triumphal arches to be seen in Rome, but only one of these is linked in any way with the name Augustus: "iuxta sanctum Laurentium in Lucina est arcus triumphalis Octaviani."[2] This is undoubtedly the arch which spanned the Via del Corso near the corner of Via della Vite, and which was known popularly in the sixteenth century as the "Arco di Portogallo."[3] It was demolished by Pope Alexander VII in 1662 (because it was an obstruction to horse racing along the Corso), and thus would have been standing in Gregory's day. However, although it did have carved reliefs, some of which are now preserved in the Palazzo dei Conservatori museum, it is again a good distance from

---

[22-1] The relevant bibliography from which the foregoing information has been extracted includes O. Richter, "Die Augustusbauten auf dem Forum Romanum," *Jahrbuch des kaiserlich deutschen archaeologischen Instituts* 4 (1889), 137-162; A. Degrassi, "L'edificio dei Fasti Capitolini," *Atti della Pontificia Accademia Romana di Archeologia. Rendiconti* 21 (1946), 57-104; G. Gatti, "La ricostruzione dell' Arco di Augusto al Foro Romano," *ibid.*, 105-122; L. B. Holland, "The Triple Arch of Augustus," *American Journal of Archaeology* 50 (1946), 52-59; idem, "The Foundations of the Arch of Augustus," *American Journal of Archaeology* 57 (1953), 1-4; and G. Carettoni, "Excavations and Discoveries in the Forum Romanum and on the Palatine During the Last Fifty Years," *Journal of Roman Studies* 50 (1960), 192-203, esp. 195. For a plan and photographs of the arch see E. Nash, *Pictorial Dictionary of Ancient Rome* (Tübingen 1961), 1: 92-101.

[2] *Cod. topog.* 3: 19.

[3] See Platner-Ashby, p. 33, and Nash 1: 83-87. It was so called because in the sixteenth century the Portuguese ambassador resided in the adjoining house.

the Pantheon and in any case was not "multiplex." The "Arco di Portogallo" was either constructed in the second century AD or else it re-used Hadrianic reliefs, and the identification with Octavian/Augustus made by the author of the *Mirabilia* is perhaps due to the proximity of other monuments clearly associated with this emperor, including his mausoleum.[4] For Gregory's arch we must again look elsewhere.

Two arches are known to have existed in the more immediate vicinity of the Pantheon. The first was the monumental gate which led to the Iseum Campense, located at what is now the western end of the Piazza del Collegio Romano. It survived until the end of the sixteenth century, at which time it was known as the Arch of Camillus.[5] There is some attraction in this possibility in that its Egyptian decorations might have been misinterpreted by Gregory as scenes from the life of Cleopatra.

The more likely candidate, however, is the "Arcus Pietatis," which was situated even closer to the front of the Pantheon. Of obscure origin, it is first mentioned by this title in a document of the year 1019, and then as a topographical indication in the *Mirabilia* and other twelfth-century sources.[6] The fourteenth-century expanded version of the *Mirabilia* elaborates as to the location: "arcus Pietatis ante Sanctam Mariam Rotundam," and associates the arch with an ancient legend concerning the justice of the emperor Trajan.[7] Almost nothing is known about this arch or its decorations, but on the basis

---

[4] As suggested by Valentini-Zucchetti, *Cod. topog.* 3: 19 note 5.

[5] See G. Gatti, "Topografia dell' Iseo Campense," *Atti della Pontificia Accademia Romana di Archeologia. Rendiconti* 20 (1943-1944), 117-163, esp. 124-137; and E. Nash 1: 118. The "Arcus ad Isis" was a triple arch. The central and northern openings were demolished in 1585, and the southern arch in 1597.

[6] *Mirabilia*, cap. 22: "Ante Sanctam Mariam in Aquiro templum Aelii Hadriani et arcus Pietatis" (*Cod. topog.* 3: 49). For the other references see R. Lanciani, "Dell' arcus Pietatis," *Notizie degli Scavi* 9 (1881), 275-276; and C. Huelsen, "Intorno all' Arcus Pietatis nel Campo Marzio," *Atti della Pontificia Accademia Romana di Archeologia, Rendiconti* 4 (1925-1926), 291-303. With regard to the precise location of the arch, Lanciani placed it directly in front of the Pantheon, while Huelsen argues for a site a bit further removed, straddling the nearby Via delle Colonelle.

[7] *Cod. topog.* 3: 185-186. The legend is also mentioned by Dante in the tenth canto of the *Purgatorio*, see Huelsen, p. 291.

of this later legend it is usually suggested that it bore reliefs depicting an emperor and his troops receiving the submission of captured territories.[8] If so, it may well have been the arch noted by Gregory, who either saw it before the legend of Trajan was transferred to it, or else chose to ignore that attribution.[9] The dedication inscription which Gregory appears to quote is not known from other sources, but in any case is unlikely to be a direct transcription.[10] A hint that the arch described in this chapter might indeed date from the Augustan period is provided by his reference to the "exstantes longe tabulas" on which the statues were placed. If this description is taken to mean that the arch was not of uniform height (i.e. that the attic of the central arch rose above those of the two sides), then its appearance would be identical to the triple arch of Augustus of 19 BC, which was constructed in precisely this fashion.[11] Later triumphal arches (for example those of Septimius Severus and Constantine) normally had attics of uniform height.

23

Presumably among these several other triumphal arches ("alios archus triumphales plures") are those which still stand in Rome today.

[8] For example Lanciani, p. 275; "Quest' arco trionfale ... era ornato di rilievi rappresentanti provincie o nazioni, in atto di supplicare e di chieder mercè all' augusto conquistatore."

[9] Rushforth, pp. 37-40, identified Gregory's arch with this "Arcus Pietatis," which he believed was the arch constructed for Augustus after the Battle of Actium. The subsequent discovery of the base of the earlier Augustan arch in the Forum, where it was also placed by Dio Cassius, now renders his hypothesis unlikely. The true identity of the "Arcus Pietatis" remains to be established.

[10] Rushforth, p. 39, is dubious of the wording as being possible for an Augustan inscription, since no reference is made to the Senate, and "regnum" is used instead of "imperium." Huelsen, p. 294 note 3, dismisses entirely "una iscrizione non veduta da nessun altro e che per la sua forma si riconosce falsa."

[11] For a reconstruction of the Arch of Augustus see E. Nash vol. 1, pl. 102.

24

Magnus Pompeius is Gnaeus Pompeius Magnus (106-48 BC), better known as Pompey, whose defeat of Mithridates, king of Pontus, resulted in the celebration of his third triumph in 61 BC. It seems unlikely that an arch was erected to honour this occasion, since the practice was not normal until the reign of Augustus, and there is no reference to it in any classical source.[1] Gregory provides no clue as to the geographical location.

It should perhaps be noted that his statement regarding Sulla is largely inaccurate. He did conduct a war against Mithridates in 87-86 BC, but instead of suffering defeat was entirely successful in forcing his foe back across the Aegean into Asia Minor. The details are given in his biography written by Plutarch.[2]

25

Gregory informs us that there are five triumphal columns in Rome which, he says, have hollow interiors and thus resemble chimneys. He then proceeds to describe one such column, which has narrative scenes carved on its exterior. He identifies these as depicting the deeds of Fabricius (Gaius Fabricius Luscinus, consul in 282 and 278 BC), who campaigned in southern Italy against Pyrrhus. Of all the triumphal and commemorative columns which were erected in ancient Rome, only three now survive: those of Trajan (AD 113),

---

[24.1] Rushforth, p. 40, decides to trust Gregory's identification and suggests that such an arch may well have stood in the vicinity of the Campus Martius, but this possibility is rejected by Platner-Ashby, pp. 42-43. There is also a curious reference to a "Pompeii arcus" in a letter of Petrarch (*Cod. topog.* 4: 8), and in the mid-fourteenth century poem *Dittamondo* of Fazio degli Uberti (*Cod. topog.* 4: 61).

[2] As Gregory seems very familiar with Lucan's *De bello civili*, he may have been influenced by Pompey's speech to his troops (2. 580-582) in which he boasts of having been more successful than Sulla against the king of Pontus.

Marcus Aurelius Antoninus (AD 193), and Phocas (AD 608).[1] Of these, only the two of the second century are hollow and have carved reliefs, and it is to one of these that Gregory undoubtedly refers. Both triumphal columns were well-known landmarks in medieval Rome. The column of Marcus Aurelius was the property of the nearby church of S. Silvestro in Capite at least as early as the mid-tenth century,[2] and a public notice to this effect was set up by the abbot Peter in the year 1119.[3] In 1162 the column of Trajan was placed under the protection of the recently revived Roman Senate, in order that it should remain "whole and undamaged as long as the world shall last."[4] Both monuments are mentioned and correctly identified in the Einsiedeln Itinerary[5] and the *Mirabilia*,[6] with the latter text even supplying figures for the height, the number of steps, and the number of "windows." In the light of this obvious familiarity it is surprising to find Gregory identifying his column with Fabricius. No monuments are known to have commemorated this military leader of the third century BC, and no other triumphal columns of the Trajanic type are known to have been erected in Rome.

Rushforth (pp. 41-42) has identified the column in question with that of Marcus Aurelius on the basis of Gregory's statement that it

---

[25.1] For bibliography see E. Nash, *Pictorial Dictionary of Ancient Rome* (Tübingen 1961), 1: 276, 280, 283. The history of free-standing column monuments has been examined by Lise Vogel, *The Column of Antoninus Pius* (Cambridge, Mass., 1973), pp. 23-31. Since at least part of the column of Antoninus Pius, the base of which is now in the Vatican Museum, was visible throughout the Middle Ages, it may have been one of the five which our author has in mind.

[2] Possession is confirmed in a bull of Pope John XII (8 March 962): "Iterumque columpna maiure marmorea in integra, que dicitur Antonina, sculpita ut videtur esse per omnia ..." The complete text is published by V. Federici, "Regesto del monastero di S. Silvestro de Capite," *Archivio della R. Società Romana di Storia Patria* 22 (1899), 213-300, esp. 269.

[3] Vincenzo Forcella, *Iscrizioni delle chiese e d'altri edifici a Roma dal secolo XI fino ai giorni nostri* 9 (Rome 1877), 79 no. 149. The inscription survives in the atrium of S. Silvestro.

[4] The decree is published by Pierluigi Galletti, *Del primicero della santa sede apostolica* (Rome 1776), pp. 323-324. The twelfth-century senators could not have envisioned how difficult a task this would be in the twentieth century with its traffic and air pollution!

[5] *Cod. topog.* 2: 181, 186, 177, 195.

[6] *Cod. topog.* 3: 31.

is the tallest in Rome. In actual fact, the two columns are of equal height (100 Roman feet), but that of Marcus Aurelius stood on a higher base, and the *Mirabilia* credits it with an advantage of thirty-seven feet.[7] This identification is largely confirmed by a reference in the mid-fourteenth-century *Polistoria* of Giovanni Cavallini de Cerronibus. In this text the column of the emperor "Antonius" is said to be carved with images depicting the most famous and virtuous Romans and their deeds. Among those in this category who are then cited by name is Fabricius.[8] Thus it would appear that while there was little doubt in medieval Rome as to the identification of the column, there was less certainty with regard to the interpretation of the reliefs. Gregory seems to have heard a story similar to that told in the *Polistoria*, and perhaps fastened on the name of Fabricius because of the reference to his moral virtue in what appears to have been his favourite Latin author, Lucan (*De bello civili* 3. 160).[9] He does admit that he has not yet had time to investigate the columns properly.

This chapter is also one of the most frustrating for anyone curious to learn more particulars about Gregory's origin. As was first noted by M.R. James (p. 541), a word has probably been lost in our manuscript copy of the text: the name of the place to which Gregory is returning.

26

Gregory now returns to the subject of triumphal arches to describe one which he says had been erected to commemorate the victory of Scipio (Publius Cornelius Scipio Africanus) over Hannibal. Again no topographical information is provided. The story as narrated appears to be a strange mixture of fact and fancy, perhaps an attempt to

---

[7] 175 feet, as opposed to 138 for the Column of Trajan. For the base see C. Caprino et al., *La Colonna di Marco Aurelio* (Rome 1955), pp. 22-28. The present arrangement is the work of Domenico Fontana in 1589.

[8] For Cavallini and his *Polistoria* see *Cod. topog.* 4: 11-19. The relevant section of lib. 8, cap. 3 is omitted by Valentini-Zucchetti but published by A. Graf, *Roma nella memoria e nelle immaginazioni del medio evo* (Turin 1915), pp. 114-115.

[9] This is the fifth quotation from this source. Perhaps it was the book which Gregory had at hand, as reading matter for the journey.

relate the carved reliefs which he had seen to what he knew of the lives of Hannibal and Scipio from Livy or some other historian. Livy does record that Scipio constructed an arch on the Capitoline hill in 190 BC (37.iii.7), which was decorated with statuary. Its fate is unknown, but there is no suggestion that it was a triumphal arch to commemorate his defeat of Hannibal at Zama (202 BC) or the latter's final demise. In any event, Hannibal's suicide took place some years later, in 183.

Rushforth has suggested that the arch which Gregory describes in this passage is none other than the Arch of Constantine, noting that a large dog appears in the first of the hunting-scene medallions.[1] Valentini-Zucchetti have dismissed this idea as "poco probabile,"[2] but Rushforth's approach—namely to put faith in Gregory's statements of what he actually saw, and give less credence to his identifications of figures and monuments—appears to be the most sensible. The only other medieval reference to an Arch of Scipio occurs in a list of arches in the mid-fourteenth-century poem, *Dittamondo*, of Fazio degli Uberti.[3]

27

The pyramid which Gregory saw near the Castel Sant' Angelo was widely believed to contain the remains of the city's legendary founder, Romulus. First described as the "meta que vocatur Memoria Romuli" in a papal bull of Leo IX in 1053,[1] its usual medieval appellation was simply the "Meta Romuli." This is the term used in the *Mirabilia*, which also records that in the early Middle Ages stone slabs had been removed from the structure to pave the atrium and steps of the

---

[26-1] Rushforth, p. 41.
[2] *Cod. topog.* 3: 163 note 3.
[3] *Cod. topog.* 4: 61.

[27-1] L. Schiaparelli, "Le carte antiche dell' archivio Capitolare di S. Pietro in Vaticano." *Archivio della R. Società Romana di Storia Patria* 24 (1901), 393-496, esp. 472. For the term "meta," which is used in Vitruvius's *De architectura*, see M. Demus-Quatember, *Est et Alia Pyramis* (Vienna 1974), pp. 21-26.

nearby church of St. Peter's.[2] The pyramid was largely demolished in 1499, when Pope Alexander VI ordered the opening of a new street from the Tiber to the Vatican in preparation for the 1500 Jubilee,[3] and excavations undertaken in the Via della Conciliazione in 1948-1949 revealed its base.[4] Nothing is known about its original occupant or date of construction, but like its extant counterpart on the other side of the city (the "Meta Remi," see ch. 28), it may well have belonged to the Augustan period of the late first century BC, a time of considerable Egyptian influence.

Because of the belief that the apostle Peter had been crucified in this part of Rome, "inter duas metas" (of which this pyramid was one), it frequently appeared in medieval and early Renaissance illustrations of this event, among them Giotto's Stefaneschi altarpiece (now in the Vatican Pinacoteca) and the bronze doors of St. Peter's by Antonio Filarete.[5]

The legend that the pyramid had originally been a hill of grain, transformed into stone when Nero attempted to sieze it from St. Peter, is not known from other sources. Gregory dismisses it contemptuously as being typical of the silly tales which circulated among the pilgrims visiting the city. It is interesting to note that the medieval mind took a curiously similar view of the great pyramids in Egypt, believing them to be the granaries built by Joseph in preparation for the seven years of famine (cf. Genesis 41). This view was already current in western Europe in late antiquity, and is recorded in the sixth century

---

[2] *Mirabilia*, cap. 20: "In Naumachia est sepulchrum Romuli, quod vocatur Meta, quae fuit miro lapide tabulata, ex quibus factum est pavimentum paradisi et graduum Sancti Petri." (*Cod. topog.* 3: 45).

[3] The details are recorded in a letter of 3 May 1499, preserved in the Biblioteca Capitolare at Lucca (cod. 555), see B.M. Peebles, "La 'Meta Romuli' e una lettera di Michele Ferno," *Atti della Pontificia Accademia Romana di Archeologia. Rendiconti* 12 (1936), 21-63.

[4] See Guglielmo Gatti, "Scavi e scoperte in Via della Conciliazione," *Fasti Archaeologici* 4 (1951), 359-360, no. 3771. The site had earlier been determined by C. Huelsen, "Il Gaianum e la Naumachia Vaticana," *Dissertazioni della Pontificia Accademia Romana di Archeologia* ser. 2, t. 8 (1903), 353-387, esp. 383-387.

[5] A list of such works is published by Peebles as an appendix, pp. 51-63. See also J.M. Huskinson, "The Crucifixion of St. Peter: a Fifteenth-Century Topographical Problem," *Journal of the Warburg and Courtauld Institutes* 32 (1969), 135-161, and M. Demus-Quatember, *Est et Alia Pyramis*.

by Gregory of Tours.[6] In the early thirteenth century, more or less contemporary with the *Narracio*, it was expressed visually in the mosaic decorations of the narthex of San Marco in Venice.[7] A similar view of the Roman pyramids could easily account for the pilgrims' story.

28

Probably this is the large pyramid tomb of Gaius Cestius Epulo, a senator in the time of the emperor Augustus, which was constructed on the via Ostiensis. In the third century AD it was incorporated into the perimeter of the Aurelian walls, and it stands to this day, restored by Pope Alexander VII in 1663.[1] In the Middle Ages it was generally referred to as the tomb of Remus,[2] in an obvious parallel to the tomb of Romulus just discussed. There is no evident reason why Gregory should refer to the gate as the Latina, or why he should identify the occupant of the tomb as Augustus. There is no mention of the emperor in the inscriptions.[3]

29

The object to which Gregory refers is the granite obelisk which now stands in St. Peter's Square, the only one of the Egyptian obelisks brought to Rome in the classical period which remained standing throughout the Middle Ages. Its history is long and most curious.[1] Probably originating from Heliopolis, although the absence of hiero-

---

[6] Gregory of Tours, *Historia Francorum* 1. 10. In the ninth century it is repeated by the Irish monk Dicuil in his *De mensura orbis terrae*, and in the account of the travels of the monk Bernard: see John Wilkinson, *Jerusalem Pilgrims* (Warminster 1977), pp. 139, 142.

[7] Otto Demus, *The Mosaics of San Marco in Venice. II: The Thirteenth Century* (Chicago 1984), pp. 136-137 and pls. 291, 295.

[28.1] For description, measurements and bibliography see Platner-Ashby, p. 478, and E. Nash, *Pictorial Dictionary of Ancient Rome* (Tübingen 1962), 2: 321.

[2] For example the *Mirabilia*, cap. 2: "porta Capena, quae vocatur Sancti Pauli iuxta sepulchrum Remi" (*Cod. topog.* 3: 17).

[3] *Corpus Inscriptionum Latinarum* 6: no. 1374.

[29.1] The principal recent studies are by Cesare d'Onofrio, *Gli Obelischi di Roma*, 2nd ed. (Rome 1967), and Erik Iversen, *Obelisks in Exile I: The Obelisks of Rome* (Copenhagen 1968).

glyphic inscriptions leaves its provenance in some doubt, it was first moved shortly after 30 BC to Alexandria, where it was set up by the prefect Cornelius Gallus in the Forum Iulium. Its first inscription, in bronze letters which were attached individually to the base, recorded this event.[2] The second inscription, still preserved, was probably added in the time of the emperor Tiberius, and refers both to Tiberius and to the deified Augustus: DIVO CAESARI DIVI IVLII F. AVGVSTO TI. CAESARI DIVI AVGVSTI F. AVGVSTO SACRVM.[3] In AD 37 it was brought from Alexandria to Rome by the emperor Caligula, and set up on the spina of the Vatican circus, where it remained until 1586.[4] Its removal to Rome is mentioned by Pliny in his *Natural History*: "An especially wonderful fir was seen in the ship which brought from Egypt at the order of the emperor Gaius the obelisk erected in the Vatican Circus and four shafts of the same stone to serve as its base."[5] Plans to move it yet again were begun in the fifteenth century under Pope Nicholas V (1447-1455), but were not fulfilled until the reign of Sixtus V (1585-1590) who entrusted the task to Domenico Fontana. The transfer to the present site in front of St. Peter's was accomplished in the period between April and September 1586.[6]

[2] The inscription, long since lost, has been brilliantly reconstructed on the basis of the holes by which the letters were attached, see Filippo Magi, "Le iscrizioni recentemente scoperte sull' obelisco vaticano," *Studi Romani* 11 (1963), 50-56.

[3] *Corpus Inscriptionum Latinarum* (Berlin 1876), vol. 6.1, no. 882. The argument that this belongs to the reign of Tiberius, and not to that of his successor Caligula, is presented by Iversen, pp. 20-21.

[4] The original position, to the south of the present nave of St. Peter's in the Piazza dei Protomartiri, is marked by an inscription set in the pavement. In 1959 excavations at this spot revealed the original foundation of the obelisk, see F. Castagnoli, "Il Circo di Nerone in Vaticano," *Atti della Pontificia Accademia Romana di Archeologia. Rendiconti* 32 (1960), 97-121. Subsequent soundings have indicated the extent of the area covered by the circus, see F. Magi, "Il circo vaticano in base alle più recente scoperte. Il suo obelisco e i suoi 'carceres'," *Atti della Pontificia Accademia Romana di Archeologia. Rendiconti* 45 (1972-1973), 37-73.

[5] Pliny, *Natural History* 16. lxxvi.201. (I have used the translation of H. Rackham in the Loeb Classical Library edition of 1945.) Both Pliny (16.lxxvi.202) and Suetonius (*Lives of the Caesars* 5.xx) record that the emperor Claudius sank this ship in the harbour at Ostia to serve as the foundation for a new mole.

[6] Among the many books on the obelisk which were published at this time is Domenico Fontana's own account of the process: *Del modo tenuto in trasferire l'obelisco vaticano* (Rome 1589).

Although the base of the obelisk was partially buried in the Middle Ages, the inscription remained visible,[7] and its misinterpretation likely led to the popular belief that the gilded bronze sphere at the top contained the ashes of Julius Caesar. This identification is also given in the *Mirabilia*,[8] and was still current in the late sixteenth century. As a result, when the obelisk was displaced in 1586, the ball was removed and taken to a room in the Belvedere where it was examined by Filippo Pigafetta. He reported that it contained no human remains, only rust and earth: "la polva trovata nel pomo non fosse cenere di morto huomo, anzi ruggine caduta dal didentro di lui, mescolata con terra cotta postavi per forma, quando lo fusero."[9] Subsequently the sphere was presented by the Pope to the "conservatori," and it was used to adorn the Capitol until it entered the collection of the Palazzo dei Conservatori in the mid-nineteenth century.[10] It remains there today.

Gregory was obviously impressed, as were others, by the fact that the obelisk had been cut from a single block of stone, a feat which gave rise to the popular saying which he records:

"Si lapis est unus, dic qua sit arte levatus,
Si lapides plures, dic ubi congeries."

---

[7] It is recorded for example in the Einsiedeln Itinerary *circa* AD 800, see *Cod. topog.* 2: 165.

[8] *Mirabilia* cap. 6: "palatium Neronis, ubi est sepulchrum Iulii Caesaris" (*Cod. topog.* 3: 22); and cap. 19: "Iuxta quod est memoria Caesaris, id est agulia, ubi splendide cinis eius in suo sarcophago requiescit." (*Cod. topog.* 3: 43). The possibility proposed by A. Graf, *Roma nella Memoria e nelle Immaginazioni del Medio Evo* (Turin 1915), p. 228, and supported by Iversen, p. 23, that the confusion results from a passage in Suetonius's biography of Caesar, seems less likely than a simple misunderstanding of the words of the inscription itself. The passage in question (1. lxxxv) refers to a marble column set up in the Forum to honour Caesar after his death, but does not state, nor even imply, that it contained his ashes: "Postea solidam columnam prope viginti pedum lapidis Numidici in Foro statuit inscripsitque PARENTI PATRIAE."

[9] *Discorso di M. Filippo Pigafetta d'intorno all' historia della Aguglia, et alla ragione del muoverla* (Rome 1586), fol. B4 verso.

[10] See *A Catalogue of the Ancient Sculptures Preserved in the Municipal Collections of Rome. The Sculptures of the Palazzo dei Conservatori*, ed. H. Stuart Jones (Oxford 1926), p. 171 no. 3. It can be identified by the dents, noted by Fontana, thought to have been caused by soldiers using it for target practice, probably during the occupation of Rome in 1527.

A similar, although not identical, version of the same question is given in the fourteenth-century revised edition of the *Mirabilia*, although here it is claimed to be an inscription inscribed on the obelisk in Greek letters:[11]

"Si lapis est unus, dic qua fuit arte levatus,
Et si sunt plures, dic ubi contingui."

There is no physical evidence that such an inscription ever existed, and thus Gregory may be correct in stating that it was simply a popular saying referring to the stone. He also reports another popular opinion, which gives the height of the obelisk as 250 feet, or approximately 75 metres. In this instance he is less accurate, since the actual height is 25.37 m. (not including the base), but it is unlikely that anyone in medieval Rome could have attempted a precise calculation, and thus the figure is probably an exaggerated guess.[12]

The information that pilgrims to Rome attempted to crawl into the narrow space between the obelisk and its base, believing that they could obtain remission of their sins by doing so, is apparently unique to the *Narracio*,[13] and it provides an interesting insight into the mentality of the medieval pilgrim. This curious behaviour was presumably occasioned by the identification of the obelisk with the site of Peter's martyrdom, resulting in the popular name for it: St. Peter's needle.[14] Gregory reports that the space between the obelisk and its base was created by four bronze lions. This is also curious, because the original bronze support pieces, or astragals, which are still in use today, are clearly *not* in the form of lions nor of any other animal. The error is by no means unique to Gregory. It may be found in the writings of no less worthy an observer than Petrarch, who refers to the bronze lions in a letter written to cardinal Giovanni

---

[11] *Cod. topog.* 3: 190.

[12] Giovanni Dondi, visiting Rome *circa* 1375, records the height as 120 feet (*Cod. topog.* 4: 68).

[13] It is repeated by Higden in his *Polychronicon*, but this cannot be considered an independent testimony.

[14] Cf. the description of Rome by the Icelandic monk, Nikolas of Munkathvera, where the obelisk is similarly called "Petrs Nal," see F.P. Magoun, "The Rome of Two Northern Pilgrims: Archbishop Sigeric of Canterbury and Abbot Nikolas of Munkathvera," *Harvard Theological Review* 33 (1940), 267-289, esp. 280.

Colonna in 1337,[15] and two lions actually appear in a thirteenth-century mural illustrating the Crucifixion of St. Peter in the church of S. Piero a Grado (near Pisa).[16] There can be no question of a switch having been made at some point between the fourteenth century and 1586,[17] as this would have involved lifting the obelisk from its base. Moreover, the original curved astragals are shown in illustrations contained in the Modena and Princeton manuscripts of Johannes Marcanova's *Quaedam antiquitatum fragmenta* of 1465,[18] and again in a sixteenth-century drawing of the obelisk by Giuliano di Sangallo.[19] It is possible that their shape suggested an animal foot to medieval observers, who were accustomed to the sight of lions supporting monuments and furnishings of all sorts, and that they simply assumed that the astragals were meant to represent lions.[20] This belief may have been encouraged by the existence in the city of a second obelisk which did indeed have lion supports, although of marble not bronze: the obelisk now in the Villa Celimontana, but which until *circa* 1535 stood on the Capitoline hill beside the side entrance to the church of S. Maria in Aracoeli. The date of its erection has not been precisely determined, although a *terminus ante quem* is provided by a clear reference to it in a diary of the year 1407.[21] D'Onofrio has linked

---

[15] *Cod. topog.* 4: 8: "Hoc est saxum mirae magnitudinis aereisque leonibus innixum, divis imperatoribus sacrum, cuius in vertice Iulii Caesaris ossa quiescere fama est."

[16] See Maria Squarciapino, "L'obelisco di San Pietro a Roma e una pittura di San Pietro in Grado," *Studi Romani* 10 (1962), 167-170; and Jens Wollesen, *Die Fresken von San Piero a Grado bei Pisa* (Bad Oeynhausen 1977), pp. 67-68.

[17] As implied by Rushforth, p. 43 note 5.

[18] For the Modena manuscript (Modena, Biblioteca Estense, MS XI.G.2) see C. Huelsen, *La Roma Antica di Ciriaco d'Ancona* (Rome 1907), tav. XI. Huelsen attributes the drawings to Cyriac, although there is no evidence to support this unlikely possibility. For the version in Princeton (University Library, MS Garrett 158) see E. Lawrence, "The Illustrations of the Garrett and Modena Manuscripts of Marcanova," *Memoirs of the American Academy in Rome* 6 (1927), 127-131, pl. 28.

[19] Biblioteca Apostolica Vaticana, MS Barb. lat. 4424, fol. 70 (reproduced by Iversen, fig. 11b).

[20] See discussion by d'Onofrio, pp. 19-20, and M. Demus-Quatember, "Ricordo di Roma. Mirabilia urbis Romae und Miracula Mundi auf einem Gemälde von Martin von Heemskerck," *Römische Historische Mitteilungen* 25 (1983), 203-223, esp. 216-217.

[21] Iversen, p. 107.

it with Cola di Rienzo (AD 1347),[22] but more recently R.E. Malmstrom has argued for a date *circa* 1200 on the basis of the style of the lion supports, which he likens to those of the entrance portal of the cathedral of Città Castellana.[23] The link is tenuous, but if Gregory (and Petrarch) had seen the lion base supporting the Capitoline obelisk, they may have been more easily convinced that the bronze astragals of the other were also meant to represent lions. This might also help to explain Gregory's statement that there were "many pyramids" in Rome, and his earlier confused identification (ch. 28) of the pyramid of Gaius Cestius as the "pyramid of Augustus," since, in an obvious parallel to its Vatican counterpart, the sphere at the top of the Capitoline obelisk was believed to contain the ashes of that emperor.[24] If Malmstrom's theory about the dating is correct, this would provide further evidence to suggest that our author's visit to Rome took place in the thirteenth century as opposed to the twelfth. As the Vatican obelisk stands today, there are indeed four lions at the corners (concealing the original astragals which are still in place), but these were added in the time of Pope Sixtus V and are the work of the artist Prospero Bresciano.

Much of the chapter is devoted to an account of Caesar's assassination, probably based on imperfect recollections of the version in Suetonius's *Lives of the Caesars* (1.lxxxi-lxxxii). In Gregory's account, however, there is evident confusion between the *horuspex* Spurinna and the unnamed person who warns Caesar of the plot in a letter.[25] Also, the fateful day is given as the kalends of the month and not the ides, the number of wounds is given as twenty-four instead of twenty-three, and the Senate meeting is set on the Capitol and not

---

[22] D'Onofrio, pp. 209-215.

[23] R.E. Malmstrom, "The Twelfth Century Church of S. Maria in Capitolio and the Capitoline Obelisk," *Römisches Jahrbuch für Kunstgeschichte* 16 (1976), 1-16, esp. 12-16. Another recent study suggests that it was put up by Pope Boniface VIII for the 1300 Jubilee, see Antonio Giuliano, "Roma 1300," *Xenia* 4 (1982), 15-22. Wollesen, p. 69, argues that the Capitoline obelisk also served as the visual model for the San Piero a Grado mural.

[24] The earliest known reference to this legend occurs in 1452 (see *Cod. topog.* 4: 362), but the association of Augustus with the site of the *ara coeli* goes back to at least the sixth century, and the story of his vision is included in the *Mirabilia* (see *Cod. topog.* 3: 28-29).

[25] In the life of Caesar by Plutarch (cap. lxv), this person is identified as Artemidorus.

in the hall of Pompey's theatre. This last must have seemed perfectly reasonable to a visitor to Rome after the middle of the twelfth century, since a Roman Senate with its seat on the Capitol had been revived in the year 1143, and in the absence of any reference to this location in the historical accounts of Caesar's death, it may well indicate a *terminus post quem* for Gregory's visit.[26]

It is worth noting that Suetonius's *praenomen* is not Marius, as Gregory claims, but Gaius, and that in the *Lives of the Caesars* there is no mention whatsoever of the blows being struck with the hilts of the swords. One can only conclude that while Gregory may have ultimately known the story from Suetonius, he most certainly did not have a copy of the text at hand, and his memory, as we have seen before, was far from perfect.

Maro is Publius Vergilius Maro, better known as Virgil, and the lines which Gregory cites are from the *Eclogues* (5.56,43-44), from the story of Daphnis. The second and third lines are the epithet for Daphnis's grave, and Gregory implies that Virgil meant them for Caesar. His source is undoubtedly the commentary on Virgil by the grammarian Servius, a work widely known in the Middle Ages (cf. ch. 14), where precisely this identification is made.[27]

30

It seems likely that the four bronze lions beneath the Vatican obelisk (ch. 29) recalled to Gregory's mind another structure which stood on animal supports, and he turns once again to the text of the *De septem miraculis mundi* for the description of the famous Alexandrian lighthouse.[1] In considering the questions about the Pharos which that

---

[26] The *Mirabilia* (cap. 23) also places the event on the Capitol: "In Tarpeio templum Asilis, ubi interfectus fuit Iulius Caesar a senatu." (*Cod. topog.* 3: 52).

[27] See *Servii Grammatici qui feruntur in Vergilii Bucolica et Georgica Commentarii*, ed. G. Thilo (Leipzig 1887), pp. 59-60. The probable use of Servius was first noted by Valentini and Zucchetti, *Cod. topog.* 3: 165 note 1.

[30.1] For this text see the Introduction and the commentary on chapter 6.

text poses, he introduces Isidore of Seville's account of the manufacture of *pozzolana*,[2] but then decides that the *Narracio* is not the place "to explain miracles."

31

The large Flavian amphitheatre or "Colosseum" is correctly associated by Gregory with the emperors Vespasian and Titus.[1] It was officially opened by the latter in AD 80. Gregory is apparently the first medieval commentator to refer to it as the "palatium Titi et Vespasiani," a title normally applied in his day to the ruins of the Circus of Maxentius on the via Appia Antica.[2]

Nothing is known of the statue of the sow with her litter of thirty piglets which he claims to have seen nearby. Its identification with the sign foretold to Aeneas by the Trojan prophet Helenus (cf. Virgil, *Aeneid* 3.390-392; 8.43-45) is quite plausible, and this passage may have provided Gregory with the number of piglets. It is possible that a statue or relief carving of this theme formed part of the decoration of the nearby Temple of Venus and Rome.[3]

The theme is not unknown in Roman art. A similar statue in Parian marble of a sow and twelve piglets may be seen in the Vatican Museum.[4]

   [2] Isidore of Seville, *Etymologiae* 16.i.8.

   [31-1] For the history of the structure, see Platner-Ashby, pp. 6-11.
   [2] Cf. *Cod. topog.* 3: 22, 82, 184.
   [3] Rushforth, pp. 27-28. This double temple, constructed by the emperor Hadrian, was largely rebuilt by Maxentius after a fire in or before AD 307. For the architecture see A. Barattolo, "Nuove ricerche sull' architettura del Tempio di Venere e di Roma in età Adrianea," *Mitteilungen des deutschen archaeologischen Instituts. Roemische Abteilung* 80 (1973), 243-269. Little is known about its decoration.
   [4] See E. Visconti, *Il Museo Pio-Clementino* (Milan 1822), 8: 155-158. This statue was found on the Quirinal, and thus is unlikely to have been the piece seen

32

From the clear reference to its location in the porch of the papal palace at the Lateran, this bronze statue of a she-wolf can be identified with the well-known piece thought to date from the fifth century BC and now in the collection of the Palazzo dei Conservatori on the Capitoline. It was among the bronze statues which were donated by Pope Sixtus IV in 1471 in order to provide the initial core of the Capitoline collection.[1] The restoration of the feet, which Gregory says were broken, may have been effected in the thirteenth century, but the addition of the figures of the twins Romulus and Remus took place sometime after the transfer to the Capitol.[2] There is no evidence that such figures had been associated with this statue in antiquity.[3]

It is not known how or when the wolf came to be included among the group of bronzes at the Lateran, but it was probably there by the second half of the eighth century. At that time, in an undoubtedly conscious attempt to emulate the palace in Rome with its Constantinian associations, Charlemagne brought a similar statue to his "Lateran"

---

by Gregory. For other examples of the theme see Visconti, p. 158 note 1.

[32-1] For the wolf see W.S. Heckscher, *Sixtus IIII Aeneas Insignes Statuas Romano Populo Restituendas Censuit* (The Hague 1955); E. Stevenson, "Scoperte di antichi edifizi al Laterano," *Annali dell' Instituto Corrispondenza Archeologica* 49 (1877), 332-384, esp. 375-381; E. Petersen, "Lupa capitolina," *Klio* 8 (1908), 440-456; 9 (1909), 29-47; Adalbert Erler, *Lupa, Lex und Reiterstandbild im mittelalterlichen Rom* (Wiesbaden 1972), pp. 9-16; and C. Dulière, *Lupa Romana. Recherches d'iconographie et essai d'interprétation* (Brussels 1979), pp. 21-43.

[2] See A. Michaelis, "Storia della collezione Capitolina di antichità fino all' inaugurazione del museo (1734)," *Mittheilungen des kaiserlich deutschen archaeologischen Instituts. Römische Abtheilung* 6 (1891), 3-66, esp. 13. The figures of the twins were attributed to the sculptor Antonio Pollaiuolo by A. Venturi, "Romolo e Remo di Antonio Pollaiolo nella lupa capitolina," *L'Arte* 22 (1919), 133-135. The first textual reference to their presence may be the letter describing the antiquities of Rome written in 1490 by Giovanni da Tolentino, see R. Schofield, "Giovanni da Tolentino Goes to Rome: a Description of the Antiquities of Rome in 1490," *Journal of the Warburg and Courtauld Institutes* 43 (1980), 246-256, esp. 252 (but see his note 41 for a warning against the reliability of this testimony).

[3] The iconography is examined by E. Löwy, "Quesiti intorno alla Lupa Capitolina," *Studi Etruschi* 8 (1934), 77-106.

palace at Aachen.[4] The first precise references to a statue of a wolf outside the papal palace occur in texts of the tenth century, where it is called the "mother of the Romans" ("mater Romanorum"), and the "place of the wolf" is identified as a place of judgment.[5] Here sentences were pronounced and punishments administered. This function continued through to the fifteenth century, and in 1438, for example, the right hands of three men who had attempted to steal gems from a papal reliquary were cut off and nailed up beside the statue.[6]

Gregory is the only source to mention the bronze ram.

33

The bronze tablet which Gregory had difficulty deciphering is to be identified with the tablet containing the *lex de imperio Vespasiani*, the enumeration of the rights and powers of the emperor Vespasian as confirmed by the Senate and People of Rome in December of AD 69. This tablet was taken from the Lateran to the Capitoline in 1576, and is now in the collection of the Capitoline Museum.[1]

The *lex de imperio* first came to prominence in May 1347, when it was used by Cola di Rienzo as the focus of a political speech.[2] It

---

[4] See Richard Krautheimer, "The Carolingian Revival of Early Christian Architecture," *Art Bulletin* 24 (1942), 1-38, esp. 35.

[5] The two references occur in the *Chronicon* of Benedict of Mt. Soracte, and in the *De imperatoria potestate in urbe Roma libellus*, possibly by the same author. See *Il Chronicon di Benedetto*, ed. G. Zucchetti (Rome 1920), pp. 145, 199. It is presumably this tradition of the wolf as "mater Romanorum" which Gregory dismisses as "fabulosum."

[6] See F. von Duhn, "Dante e la Lupa Capitolina," *Studi Etruschi* 2 (1928), 9-14. The wolf and the hands were depicted in a mural in the Lateran basilica, as known from a drawing preserved in the Archivio Lateranense (published *ibid.*, pl. 1.2).

[33-1] The text (*Corpus Inscriptionum Latinarum* 6: 930) is studied by L. Cantarelli, "La lex de imperio Vespasiani," *Bullettino della Commissione Archeologica Comunale di Roma* 18 (1890), 194-208, 235-246.

[2] As described in the anonymous fourteenth-century *vita* of Cola, published by L. Muratori, *Antiquitates Italicae Medii Aevi* (Milan 1740), 3: 405. See also E. Duprè

is not known how it came to be at the Lateran, but like the other bronzes it may well have been taken there when the papal residence was restored in the eighth century.[3] A letter written by Cola di Rienzo to the archbishop of Prague in 1350 claims that he had rediscovered it in one of the altars of the church, where it had been "hidden" by Pope Boniface VIII (1294-1303).[4] Before Boniface's time, it was apparently on display in the porch.

Rushforth rejected this identification on the grounds that the *lex de imperio* could not have been interpreted as a "tabula prohibens peccatum," and suggested that Gregory may have seen a different tablet, containing the texts of ancient laws such as the Law of the Twelve Tables.[5] However, his objection is not warranted. It appears that few, if indeed any, in the late Middle Ages were capable of reading the tablet, whose script had long since passed out of date, and thus few had any clear idea of its contents. This is admitted by Gregory himself, and also explicitly stated by the anonymous biographer of Cola who, describing the events of 1347, says that no one knew how to read or to interpret the tablet.[6] Gregory's interpretation is paralleled by that of the thirteenth-century Bolognese jurist, Odofredo, who was also unable to read the text but concluded that it must contain the Law of the Twelve Tables.[7] Presumably this was the popular view.

Theseider, *Roma dal Comune di popolo alla Signoria pontificia (1252-1377)* (Bologna 1952), pp. 537-538.

[3] For the significance of the tablet to the papal claims of temporal power see Adalbert Erler, *Lupa, Lex und Reiterstandbild im mittelalterlichen Rom* (Wiesbaden 1972), pp. 16-20, and R. Krautheimer, *Rome: Profile of a City, 312-1308* (Princeton 1980), p. 193. For the political context of the return of the papal residence to the Lateran in the mid eighth century see P. Verzone, "La distruzione dei palazzi imperiali di Roma e di Ravenna e la ristrutturazione del palazzo Lateranense nel IX secolo nei rapporti con quello di Costantinopoli," *Roma e l'Età Carolingia* (Rome 1976), pp. 39-54.

[4] Because of Boniface's own "odium imperii." For the letter see *Epistolario di Cola di Rienzo*, ed. A. Gabrielli (Rome 1890), pp. 144-179, esp. 165. Cola set up the tablet "in order that it may be seen and read by everyone."

[5] Rushforth, p. 29.

[6] V. *supra* note 2.

[7] See E. Duprè Theseider, p. 537.

It seems strange to us in the twentieth century that these elegant capital letters can have posed any difficulty to a medieval viewer, but such was evidently indeed the case. An interesting parallel is provided by a Carolingian *Aratea* manuscript (Leiden, University Library, Cod. lat. Voss. 79), where the rustic capitals of the ninth century were transliterated into readable script by a thirteenth-century scribe. Erwin Panofsky, noting this odd occurrence, suggests that it can only have been done "because he evidently thought that the Carolingian 'Rustic Capital' would stump his contemporaries, as well as future generations."[8] One can also compare the comment of the fourteenth-century humanist physician, Giovanni Dondi, on the inscription carved on the Arch of Constantine: "multe litere sculpte, sed difficiliter leguntur."[9]

---

[8] E. Panofsky, *Renaissance and Renascences in Western Art* (New York 1969), p. 107.

[9] *Cod. topog.* 4: 70.

Bibliography

Ackerman, James S. "Marcus Aurelius on the Capitoline Hill." *Renaissance News* 10 (1957), 69-75.
Adhémar, Jean. *Influences antiques dans l'art du moyen-âge français*. London, 1939.
Adriani, Maurilio. "Paganesimo e cristianesimo nei 'Mirabilia urbis Romae'." *Studi Romani* 8 (1960), 535-552.
Amadei, Emma. *Le Torri di Roma*. 3rd ed. Rome, 1969.
Ashby, Thomas. *The Aqueducts of Ancient Rome*. Oxford, 1935.
——. "The Classical Topography of the Roman Campagna." *Papers of the British School at Rome* 1 (1902), 125-285; 3 (1906), 1-212; 4 (1907), 1-159.

Babut, Ernest. "Les statues équestres du Forum." *Mélanges d'Archéologie et d'Histoire* 20 (1900), 209-222.
Barattolo, A. "Nuove ricerche sull' architettura del Tempio di Venere e di Roma in età Adrianea." *Mitteilungen des deutschen archaeologischen Instituts. Roemische Abteilung* 80 (1973), 243-269.
Bartoli, Alfonso. "Scoperta dell' oratorio e del monastero di S. Cesario sul Palatino." *Nuovo Bullettino di Archeologia Cristiana* 13 (1907), 191-204.
Bede, the Venerable. *Bede's Ecclesiastical History of the English People*. Ed. B. Colgrave and R.A.B. Mynors. Oxford, 1969.
Benedict. *Il Chronicon di Benedetto*. Ed. G. Zucchetti. Rome, 1920.
Benson, Robert. "Political 'Renovatio': Two Models from Roman Antiquity." In *Renaissance and Renewal in the Twelfth Century*, ed. Robert Benson and Giles Constable, pp. 339-386. Oxford, 1982.
Bloch, Herbert. "Der Autor der 'Graphia aureae urbis Romae'." *Deutsches Archiv für Erforschung des Mittelalters* 40 (1984), 55-175.
——. "The New Fascination with Ancient Rome." In *Renaissance and Renewal in the Twelfth Century*, ed. Robert Benson and Giles Constable, pp. 616-636. Oxford, 1982.
Borchardt, Paul. "The Sculpture in Front of the Lateran as Described by Benjamin of Tudela and Magister Gregorius." *Journal of Roman Studies* 26 (1936), 68-70.
Brentano, Robert. *Rome before Avignon*. London, 1974.

Buddensieg, Tilmann. "Criticism and Praise of the Pantheon in the Middle Ages and the Renaissance." In *Classical Influences on European Culture, A.D. 500-1500*, ed. R. Bolgar, pp. 259-267. Cambridge, 1971.
——. "Criticism of Ancient Architecture in the Sixteenth and Seventeenth Centuries." In *Classical Influences on European Culture, A.D. 1500-1700*, ed. R. Bolgar, pp. 335-348. Cambridge, 1976.
——. "Die Statuenstiftung Sixtus' IV. im Jahre 1471." *Römisches Jahrbuch für Kunstgeschichte* 20 (1983), 33-73.
——. "Gregory the Great, the Destroyer of Pagan Idols. The History of a Medieval Legend Concerning the Decline of Ancient Art and Literature." *Journal of the Warburg and Courtauld Institutes* 28 (1965), 44-65.

Cantarelli, L. "La lex de impero Vespasiani." *Bullettino della Commissione Archeologica Comunale di Roma* 18 (1890), 194-208, 235-246.
Canter, Howard. "The Venerable Bede and the Colosseum." *Transactions and Proceedings of the American Philological Association* 61 (1930), 150-164.
Caprino, C. et al. *La Colonna di Marco Aurelio*. Rome, 1955.
Carettoni, Gianfilippo. "Excavations and Discoveries in the Forum Romanum and on the Palatine During the Last Fifty Years." *Journal of Roman Studies* 50 (1960), 192-203.
——. "Il Palatino nel Medioevo." *Studi Romani* 9 (1961), 508-518.
Castagnoli, F. "Il Circo di Nerone in Vaticano." *Atti della Pontificia Accademia Romana di Archeologia. Rendiconti* 32 (1960), 97-121.
A Catalogue of the Ancient Sculptures Preserved in the Municipal Collections of Rome. The Sculptures of the Museo Capitolino. Ed. H. Stuart Jones. Oxford, 1912.
A Catalogue of the Ancient Sculptures Preserved in the Municipal Collections of Rome. The Sculptures of the Palazzo dei Conservatori. Ed. H. Stuart Jones. Oxford, 1926.
Cecchelli, Carlo. "Per la storia antica e medioevale di Castel S. Angelo." *Archivio della Società Romana di Storia Patria* 74 (1951), 27-67.
Cilento, Nicola. "Sulla tradizione della 'Salvatio civium': la magica tutela della città medievale." In *Roma anno 1300*, Ed. Angiola Maria Romanini, pp. 695-705. Rome, 1983.
Coarelli, Filippo. *Guida Archeologica di Roma*. 3rd ed. Verona, 1980.
Cocke, Richard. "Masaccio and the Spinario, Piero and the Pothos: Observations on the Reception of the Antique in Renaissance Painting." *Zeitschrift für Kunstgeschichte* 43 (1980), 21-32.
Corpus Inscriptionum Latinarum. Berlin, 1869- .

Davis-Weyer, Caecilia. *Early Medieval Art. Sources and Documents.* Englewood Cliffs, N.J., 1971.
De Beer, E.S. "The Development of the Guide Book Until the Early Nineteenth Century." *Journal of the British Archaeological Association* 3rd ser., 15 (1952), 35-46.
De Boüard, A. "Gli antichi marmi di Roma nel medio evo." *Archivio della R. Società Romana di Storia Patria* 34 (1911), 239-245.
Deér, József. *The Dynastic Porphyry Tombs of the Norman Period in Sicily.* Cambridge, Mass., 1959.
Degrassi, A. "L'edificio dei Fasti Capitolini." *Atti della Pontificia Accademia Romana di Archeologia. Rendiconti* 21 (1946), 57-104.
Delahaye, Hippolyte. "L'amphithéâtre Flavien et ses environs dans les textes hagiographiques." *Analecta Bollandiana* 16 (1897), 209-252.
———. "Recherches sur le légendier romain." *Analecta Bollandiana* 51 (1933), 34-98.
Demus, Otto. *The Mosaics of San Marco in Venice II: the Thirteenth Century.* Chicago, 1984.
Demus-Quatember, Margaretha. *Est et Alia Pyramis.* Vienna, 1974.
———. "Ricordo di Roma. Mirabilia urbis Romae und Miracula Mundi auf einem Gemälde von Martin van Heemskerck." *Römische Historische Mitteilungen* 25 (1983), 203-223.
———. "Zur Weltwunderliste des Pseudo-Beda und ihren Beziehungen zu Rom." *Römische Historische Mitteilungen* 12 (1970), 67-92.
Deonna, W. "Le Béllerophon de Smyrne et l'aimant magique." *Revue Archéologique* IV ser., 24 (1914), 102-106.
De Rossi, G.B. and G. Gatti. "Miscellanea di notizie bibliografiche e critiche per la topografia e la storia dei monumenti di Roma." *Bullettino della Commissione Archeologica Comunale di Roma* 14 (1886), 240-247, 345-356.
D'Haenens, Albert. "Aller à Rome au Moyen Âge." *Bulletin de l'Institut Historique Belge de Rome* 50 (1980), 93-129.
Dodwell, Barbara. *The Charters of Norwich Cathedral Priory.* London, 1974.
D'Onofrio, Cesare. *Castel S. Angelo e Borgo tra Roma e Papato.* Rome, 1978.
———. *Gli Obelischi di Roma.* 2nd ed. Rome, 1967.
Duchesne, Louis. "L'auteur des Mirabilia." *Mélanges d'Archéologie et d'Histoire* 24 (1904), 479-489.
———. "Notes sur la topographie de Rome au moyen âge." *Mélanges d'Archéologie et d'Histoire* 9 (1889), 346-362.
Dulière, Cécile. *Lupa Romana. Recherches d'iconographie et essai d'interprétation.* Brussels, 1979.

Duprè Theseider, Eugenio. *Roma dal Comune die popolo alla Signoria pontificia (1252-1377)*. Bologna, 1952.
Egger, Gerhart. "Probleme konstantinischen Plastik." *Jahrbuch der Kunsthistorischen Sammlungen in Wien* 62 (1966), 71-102.
Erler, Adalbert. *Lupa, Lex und Reiterstandbild im mittelalterlichen Rom*. Wiesbaden, 1972.
Esch, A. "Spolien. Zur Wiederverwendung antiken Baustücke und Skulpturen im mittelalterlichen Italien." *Archiv für Kulturgeschichte* 51 (1969), 1-64.
Evans, Harold. "Nero's 'Arcus Caelimonti'." *American Journal of Archaeology* 87 (1983), 392-399.

Fedele, Pietro. "Sul commercio delle antichità in Roma nel XII secolo." *Archivio della R. Società Romana di Storia Patria* 32 (1909), 465-470.
Federici, Vincenzo. "Regesto del monastero di S. Silvestro de Capite." *Archivio della R. Società Romana di Storia Patria* 22 (1899), 213-300.
Fehl, Philip. "The Placement of the Equestrian Statue of Marcus Aurelius in the Middle Ages." *Journal of the Warburg and Courtauld Institutes* 37 (1974), 362-367.
Fontana, Domenico. *Del modo tenuto in trasferire l'obelisco vaticano*. Rome, 1589.
Forcella, Vincenzo. *Iscrizioni delle chiese e d'altri edifici a Roma dal secolo XI fino ai giorni nostri*. Rome, 1869-1884.
Fossi, G. "La représentation de l'Antiquité dans la sculpture romane et une figuration classique: le tireur d'épine." In *La Représentation de l'Antiquité au Moyen Âge*, pp. 299-324. Vienne, 1982.
Fronto, Marcus Cornelius. *The Correspondence of Marcus Cornelius Fronto*. Ed. C.R. Haines. London, 1955.

Gagé, Jean. "Le Colosse et la fortune de Rome." *Mélanges d'Archéologie et d'Histoire* 45 (1928), 106-122.
Galletti, Pierluigi. *Del primicero della santa sede apostolica*. Rome, 1776.
Gatti, Guglielmo. "La ricostruzione dell' Arco di Augusto al Foro Romano." *Atti della Pontificia Accademia Romana di Archeologia. Rendiconti* 21 (1946), 105-122.
———. "Scavi e scoperte in Via della Conciliazione." *Fasti Archaeologici* 4 (1951), 359-360.
———. . "Topografia dell' Iseo Campense." *Atti della Pontificia Accademia Romana di Archeologia. Rendiconti* 20 (1943-1944), 117-163.
Giuliano, Antonio. "Roma 1300." *Xenia* 4 (1982), 15-22.

Graf, Arturo. *Roma nella memoria e nelle immaginazioni del medio evo.* Turin, 1915.

Gregorius. *Narracio de Mirabilibus urbis Romae.* Ed. R.B.C. Huygens. Leiden, 1970.

Grierson, Philip. *Catalogue of the Byzantine Coins in the Dumbarton Oaks Collection.* Vol. 3. Washington, 1973.

Guidi, Ignazio. "La descrizione di Roma nei geografi arabi." *Archivio della R. Società Romana di Storia Patria* 1 (1878), 173-218.

Haskell, Francis and Nicholas Penny. *Taste and the Antique.* New Haven, 1981.

Haskins, Charles H. *The Renaissance of the Twelfth Century.* Cambridge, Mass., 1927.

Heckscher, W.S. "Dornauszieher." *Reallexikon zur deutschen Kunstgeschichte* 4: 289-299. Stuttgart, 1958.

——. "Relics of Pagan Antiquity in Medieval Settings." *Journal of the Warburg and Courtauld Institutes* 1 (1937-1938), 204-220.

——. *Sixtus IIII Aeneas Insignes Statuas Romano Populo Restituendas Censuit.* The Hague, 1955.

Helbig, Wolfgang. *Guide to the Public Collections of Classical Antiquities in Rome.* Leipzig, 1895-1896.

Herklotz, Ingo. 'Sepulcra' e 'Monumenta' del Medioevo. Rome, 1985.

——. "Der Campus Lateranensis im Mittelalter." *Römisches Jahrbuch für Kunstgeschichte* 22 (1985), 1-43.

Herschel, Clemens. *The Water Supply of the City of Rome.* Boston, 1899.

Higden, Ranulf. *Polychronicon.* Ed. Churchill Babington. London, 1865.

Hildebert. *Hildeberti Cenomannensis episcopi carmina minora.* Ed. A.B. Scott. Leipzig, 1969.

Holland, L.B. "The Foundations of the Arch of Augustus." *American Journal of Archaeology* 57 (1953), 1-4.

——. "The Triple Arch of Augustus." *American Journal of Archaeology* 50 (1946), 52-59.

Huelsen, Christian. *Le Chiese di Roma nel Medio Evo.* Florence, 1927.

——. "Il Gaianum e la Naumachia Vaticana." *Dissertazioni della Pontificia Accademia Romana di Archeologia* ser. 2, t. 8 (1903), 353-387.

——. "Intorno all' Arcus Pietatis nel Campo Marzio." *Atti della Pontificia Accademia Romana di Archeologia. Rendiconti* 4 (1925-1926), 291-303.

——. "Note di topografia romana antica e medievale." *Bullettino della Commissione Archeologica Comunale di Roma* 54 (1926), 49-66.

——. *La Roma Antica di Ciriaco d'Ancona.* Rome, 1907.

——. *Das Septizonium des Septimius Severus.* Berlin, 1886.

———. "Il Tempio del Sole nella regione VII di Roma." *Bullettino della Commissione Archeologica Comunale di Roma* 23 (1895), 39-59.
Huskinson, J.M. "The Crucifixion of St. Peter: a Fifteenth-Century Topographical Problem." *Journal of the Warburg and Courtauld Institutes* 32 (1969), 135-161.
Iversen, Erik. *Obelisks in Exile I: the Obelisks of Rome*. Copenhagen, 1968.
James, Montague R. *A Descriptive Catalogue of the Manuscripts in the Library of St. Catharine's College, Cambridge*. Cambridge, 1925.
———. "Magister Gregorius de Mirabilibus urbis Romae." *English Historical Review* 32 (1917), 531-554.
John of Salisbury. *Historia Pontificalis*. Ed. R. Poole. Oxford, 1927.
———. *Memoirs of the Papal Court*. Tr. M. Chibnall. London, 1956.
Jones, Charles W. *Bedae Pseudepigrapha: Scientific Writings Falsely Attributed to Bede*. Ithaca, N.Y., 1939.

Katermaa, Aino. "Le casetorri medievali di Roma." *Opuscula Instituti Romani Finlandiae* 1 (1981), 41-55.
Kehr, Paul F. *Italia Pontificia*. Berlin, 1906.
Kitzinger, Ernst. "The Arts as Aspects of a Renaissance: Rome and Italy." In *Renaissance and Renewal in the Twelfth Century*, ed. Robert Benson and Giles Constable, pp. 637-670. Oxford, 1982.
Krautheimer, Richard. "The Carolingian Revival of Early Christian Architecture." *Art Bulletin* 24 (1942), 1-38.
———. *Rome: Profile of a City, 312-1308*. Princeton, 1980.

Lanciani, Rodolfo. "Dell' arcus Pietatis." *Notizie degli Scavi di Antichità* 9 (1881), 275-276.
———. "Di un frammento inedito della pianta di Roma antica riferibile alla Regione VII." *Bullettino della Commissione Archeologica Comunale di Roma* 22 (1894), 285-311.
———. "Gli edifici della prefettura urbana fra la Tellure e le terme di Tito e di Traiano." *Bullettino della Commissione Archeologica Comunale di Roma* 20 (1892), 19-37.
———. "L'Itinerario di Einsiedeln e l'Ordine di Benedetto Canonico." *Monumenti Antichi* 1 (1890-1892), 438-551.
———. *Storia degli Scavi di Roma*. Rome, 1902.
La Rocca, Eugenio. "Sulle vicende del Marco Aurelio dal 1912 al 1980." *Studi Romani* 29 (1981), 56-60.
Lauer, Philippe. *Le Palais de Latran*. Paris, 1911.
Lawrence, Elizabeth. "The Illustrations of the Garrett and Modena Manuscripts of Marcanova." *Memoirs of the American Academy in Rome* 6 (1927), 127-131.
Liber Pontificalis. Ed. L. Duchesne. Paris, 1886.

Licht, Kjeld. *The Rotunda in Rome*. Copenhagen, 1968.
Löwy, Emanuel. "Quesiti intorno alla Lupa Capitolina." *Studi Etruschi* 8 (1934), 77-106.
MacDonald, William. *The Pantheon*. London, 1976.
Magi, Filippo. "Il circo vaticano in base alle più recente scoperte. Il suo obelisco e i suoi 'carceres'." *Atti della Pontificia Accademia Romana di Archeologia. Rendiconti* 45 (1972-1973), 37-73.
——. "Le iscrizioni recentemente scoperte sull' obelisco vaticano." *Studi Romani* 11 (1963), 50-56.
Magoun, Francis P. "The Rome of Two Northern Pilgrims: Archbishop Sigeric of Canterbury and Abbot Nikolas of Munkathvera." *Harvard Theological Review* 33 (1940), 267-289.
Malmstrom, R.E. "The Twelfth Century Church of S. Maria in Capitolio and the Capitoline Obelisk." *Römisches Jahrbuch für Kunstgeschichte* 16 (1976), 1-16.
Mango, Cyril. "Antique Statuary and the Byzantine Beholder." *Dumbarton Oaks Papers* 17 (1963), 53-75.
Manitius, Maximilianus. *Geschichte der lateinischen Litteratur des Mittelalters*. Munich, 1931.
Marucchi, Orazio. "I leoni del re Nektanebo." *Bullettino della Commissione Archeologica Comunale di Roma* 18 (1890), 307-325.
Michaelis, A. "Le antichità della città di Roma descritte da Nicolau Muffel." *Mitteilungen des kaiserlich deutschen archaeologischen Instituts. Römische Abteilung* 3 (1888), 254-276.
——. "Monte Cavallo." *Mitteilungen des deutschen Archaeologischen Instituts. Römische Abteilung* 13 (1898), 248-274.
——. "Storia della collezione Capitolina di antichità fino all' inaugurazione del museo (1734)." *Mitteilungen des deutschen archaeologischen Instituts. Römische Abteilung* 6 (1891), 3-66.
Monumenta Germaniae Historica. Scriptores Rerum Langobardicarum et Italicarum. Hannover, 1878.
Moore, Frank. "The Gilt-Bronze Tiles of the Pantheon." *American Journal of Archaeology* 3 (1899), 40-43.
Mouriki, Doula. "The Theme of the 'Spinario' in Byzantine Art." *Deltion tēs Christianikēs Archaiologikēs Heraireias* 6 (1970-1972), 53-66.
Muratori, Lodovico. *Antiquitates Italicae Medii Aevi*. Vol. 3. Milan, 1740.
Mynors, Roger A.B. "The Latin Classics Known to Boston of Bury." In *Fritz Saxl (1890-1948). A Volume of Memorial Essays from his Friends in England*. ed. D.J. Gordon, pp. 199-217. Edinburgh, 1957.
Nash, Ernest. *Pictorial Dictionary of Ancient Rome*. Tübingen, 1961-1962.

Neckam, Alexander. *De Naturis Rerum Libri Duo.* Ed. T. Wright. London, 1863.
Nesselrath, Arnold. "Antico and Monte Cavallo." *The Burlington Magazine* 124 (1982), 353-357.
Nichols, Francis. *The Marvels of Rome.* London, 1889.
Nochles, Karl. "Die Kunst der Cosmaten und die Idee der Renovatio Romae." In *Festschrift Werner Hager,* ed. Gunther Fiensch and Max Imdahl, pp. 17-37. Recklinghausen, 1966.
Il Nuovo Teatro delle Fabbriche, et Edifici, in prospettiva di Roma Moderna. Ed. G. Rossi. Rome, 1665.
Omont, Henri. "Les sept merveilles du monde au moyen âge." *Bibliothèque de l'École des Chartes* 43 (1882), 40-59.
Osborne, John. "The Earliest Antiquarian Description of Caracalla's Sarapeum on the Quirinal Hill in Rome." *Echos du Monde Antique/Classical Views* 27 (1983), 220-225.
———. "Peter's Grain Heap: a Medieval View of the 'Meta Romuli'." *Echos du Monde Antique/Classical Views* 30 (1986), 111-118.
Panofsky, Erwin. *Abbot Suger on the Abbey Church of St. Denis and its Art Treasures.* 2nd ed. Princeton, 1979.
———. *Renaissance and Renascences in Western Art.* New York, 1972.
Paravicini Bagliani, Agostino. *Cardinali di Curia e 'Familiae' cardinalizie dal 1227 al 1254.* Padua, 1972.
Parks, George B. *The English Traveler to Italy.* Rome, 1954.
Patrologiae cursus completus, series Graeca. Ed. J. P. Migne. Paris 1857-1866.
Patrologiae cursus completus, series Latina. Ed. J.P. Migne. Paris 1844-1855.
Peebles, Bernard M. "La 'Meta Romuli' e una lettera di Michele Ferno." *Atti della Pontificia Accademia Romana di Archeologia. Rendiconti* 12 (1936), 21-63.
Petersen, E. "Lupa Capitolina." *Klio* 8 (1908), 440-456; 9 (1909), 29-47.
Pigafetta, M. *Discorso di M. Filippo Pigafetta d'intorno all' historia della Aguglia, et alla ragione del muoverla.* Rome, 1586.
Platner, Samuel and Thomas Ashby. *A Topographical Dictionary of Ancient Rome.* London, 1929.
Quilici, Lorenzo. "La via Collatina: analisi topografico dell' antico percorso." *Bullettino della Commissione Archeologica Comunale di Roma* 79 (1963-64), 99-106.
Raby, Frederic. *A History of Secular Latin Poetry in the Middle Ages.* 2nd ed. Oxford, 1957.

Reekmans, Louis. "L'implantation monumentale chrétienne dans la zone suburbaine de Rome du IVe au IXe siècle." *Rivista di Archeologia Cristiana* 44 (1968), 173-207.

Reinach, Salomon. "Une statue de Bellérophon à Smyrne." *Revue Archéologique* IV ser., 20 (1912), 330-333.

Rerum Italicarum Scriptores. Ed. Lodovico A. Muratori. Milan, 1723-1738.

Richmond, Ian. *The City Wall of Imperial Rome*. Oxford, 1930.

Richter, O. "Die Augustusbauten auf dem Forum Romanum." *Jahrbuch des kaiserlich deutschen archaeologischen Instituts* 4 (1889), 137-162.

Rienzo, Cola di. *Epistolario di Cola di Rienzo*. Ed. A. Gabrielli. Rome, 1890.

Rodocanachi, Emmanuel. *The Roman Capitol*. London, 1906.

Ross, James B. "A Study of Twelfth-Century Interest in the Antiquities of Rome." In *Medieval and Historiographical Essays in Honor of James Westfall Thompson*, ed. James L. Cate and Eugene N. Anderson, pp. 302-331. Chicago, 1938.

Roullet, Anne. *The Egyptian and Egyptianizing Monuments of Imperial Rome*. Leiden, 1972.

Rushforth, Gordon. "Magister Gregorius de Mirabilibus urbis Romae: a New Description of Rome in the Twelfth Century." *Journal of Roman Studies* 9 (1919), 14-58.

Russell, Josiah C. *Dictionary of Writers of Thirteenth Century England*. London, 1936.

Santa Maria Scrinari, Valnea. "Scavi sotto sala Mazzoni all' ospedale di S. Giovanni in Roma. Relazione preliminare." *Atti della Pontificia Accademia Romana di Archeologia. Rendiconti* 41 (1968-1969), 167-189.

Santangelo, Maria. "Il Quirinale nell' antichità classica." *Atti della Pontificia Accademia Romana di Archeologia. Memorie* 5 (1941), 77-214.

Schiaparelli, Luigi. "Le carte antiche dell' archivio Capitolare di S. Pietro in Vaticano." *Archivio della R. Società Romana di Storia Patria* 24 (1901), 393-496.

Schofield, Richard. "Giovanni da Tolentino Goes to Rome: A Description of the Antiquities of Rome in 1490." *Journal of the Warburg and Courtauld Institutes* 43 (1980), 246-256.

Schramm, Percy E. *Kaiser, Könige und Päpste*. Stuttgart, 1968-1970.

Schweikhart, Gunter. "Von Priapus zu Coridon; Benennungen des Dornausziehers in Mittelalter und Neuzeit." *Würzburger Jahrbücher für die Altertumswissenschaft* 3 (1977), 243-252.

Servius. *Servii Grammatici qui feruntur in Vergilii Bucolica et Georgica Commentarii.* Ed. G. Thilo. Leipzig, 1887.

——. *Servii Grammatici qui feruntur in Vergilii Carmina Commentarii.* Ed. G. Thilo and H. Hagen. Leipzig, 1923.

Sims-Williams, Patrick. "William of Malmesbury and 'La Silloge Epigrafica di Cambridge'." *Archivum Historiae Pontificae* 21 (1983), 9-33.

Southern, R.W. "The Place of England in the Twelfth-Century Renaissance." *History* 45 (1960), 201-216.

——. "The Schools of Paris and the School of Chartres." In *Renaissance and Renewal in the Twelfth Century,* ed. Robert Benson and Giles Constable, pp. 113-137. Oxford, 1982.

Squarciapino, Maria. "L'obelisco di San Pietro a Roma e una pittura di San Pietro in Grado." *Studi Romani* 10 (1962), 167-170.

Stambaugh, John. *Sarapis Under the Early Ptolemies.* Leiden, 1972.

Stevenson, E. "Scoperte di antichi edifizi al Laterano." *Annali dell' Instituto Corrispondenza Archeologica* 49 (1877), 332-384.

Taylor, John. *The 'Universal Chronicle' of Ranulph Higden.* Oxford, 1966.

Tellenbach, Gerd. "La città di Roma dal ix al xii secolo vista dai contemporanei d'oltre frontiera." In *Studi storici in onore di Ottorino Bertolini,* 2: 679-734. Pisa, 1972.

Todd, Malcolm. *The Walls of Rome.* London, 1978.

Toubert, Pierre. *Les Structures du Latium Médiéval.* Rome, 1973.

Valentini, Roberto and Giuseppe Zucchetti. *Codice Topografico della Città di Roma.* Rome, 1940-1953.

Van der Straeten, Joseph. "Les chaînes de St. Pierre. Une nouvelle version de la légende." *Analecta Bollandiana* 90 (1972), 413-424.

Venturi, Adolfo. "Romolo e Remo di Antonio Pollaiolo nella lupa capitolina." *L'Arte* 22 (1919), 133-135.

Verzone, Paolo. "La distruzione dei palazzi imperiali di Roma e di Ravenna e la ristrutturazione del palazzo Lateranense nel ix secolo nei rapporti con quello di Costantinopoli." In *Roma e l'Età Carolingia,* pp. 39-54. Rome, 1976.

Visconti, E. *Il Museo Pio-Clementino.* Vol. 8. Milan, 1822.

Vogel, Lise. *The Column of Antoninus Pius.* Cambridge, Mass., 1973.

Von Duhn, F. "Dante e la Lupa Capitolina." *Studi Etruschi* 2 (1928), 9-14.

Welles, C.B. "The Discovery of Sarapis and the Foundation of Alexandria." *Historia* 11 (1962), 271-298.

Who was Who in the Roman World. Ed. Dianna Bowder. Oxford, 1980.

Wilkinson, John. *Jerusalem Pilgrims.* Warminster, 1977.

Wollesen, Jens. *Die Fresken von San Piero a Grado bei Pisa.* Bad Oeynhausen, 1977.

Zucchetti, Giuseppe. "Marco Aurelio." *Capitolium* 28 (1953), 328-332.

Index

Alexandria, Pharos of 5, 35, 94-95
Apollo Bianeus, Bath of 6, 25, 28, 58, 71
Aqueduct of Aqua Claudia 28, 68, 69-71
Aquila, house of 5, 29, 71-72
Augustus, Arch of 30-31, 79-82
Augustus, palace of 28, 68-69, 74
Augustus, pyramid of 33, 87, 88, 93

Bacchus, statue of 26, 61
Bellerophon, statue of 25, 57-58
Benjamin of Tudela 45, 50, 53, 54, 75

Castel S. Angelo 3, 19, 33, 42-43
Castor and Pollux, statues of 26, 59-60, 61
Cleopatra 30, 79
Colosseum 35, 49, 95
Colossus of Nero 4, 22-23, 48-53
Cornuti, Palace of the 4, 27, 61-65
Crescentius, Castle of, *see* Castel S. Angelo

Diocletian, Baths of 5, 27, 65-66

Einsiedeln Itinerary 38, 39, 45, 60, 65, 72, 84, 90

Fabricius, Column of 32, 83-85
Fronto, house of 5, 29, 71-72

Gates of Rome 19, 38-42

Graphia aureae urbis Romae 9, 43, 47, 50, 55, 69, 73
Gregory I, pope 6, 19, 23, 48, 50, 51, 59

Hannibal 32, 33, 85, 86
Henry of Blois 7
Heraklea, theatre at 25, 58
Higden, Ranulph 1, 2, 3, 10, 12, 13, 47, 48
Hildebert of Lavardin 8, 10, 12, 18, 38
Hippolytus, saint 6, 28, 68, 72

Innocent II, pope 8, 68
Innocent III, pope 11, 67
Isidore of Seville 12, 35, 57, 69, 95

John of Salisbury 6, 7, 51
Julius Caesar, pyramid of 6, 34, 88-94

Lateran Palace 11, 19, 36, 44, 48, 55, 58, 70, 96, 98
Lex de imperio Vespasiani 33, 97-99
Liber Pontificalis 44
Lucan 12, 18, 32, 38, 83, 85
Lupa Capitolina 5, 36, 96-97

Marcus Aurelius, statue of 3, 19-22, 43-48
Mirabilia urbis Romae 9, 39, 42, 43, 46, 47, 50, 51, 54, 55, 60, 66, 67, 69, 73, 74, 76, 77, 80, 81, 84, 86, 90, 91

Mithridates 31, 83

Neckam, Alexander 55, 56, 57, 58
Nero, palace of 29, 72-73
Nerva, palace of 29, 72-73

Octavian, palace of 29, 72-74
Otto of Tonengo 14
Ovid 29, 43, 59, 74

Pallas, Temple of 27-28, 66-68
Pantheon 5, 6, 7, 9, 29, 43, 55, 76-79, 80-81
Pompey, arch of 31, 83
Priapus, statue of, *see* Spinario
Pseudo-Bede, *De septem miraculis mundi* 4, 5, 12, 51, 52, 55, 56, 57, 58, 94
Pyrrhus 32, 83

Quintus Quirinus 19, 21-22, 47

Romulus, pyramid of 5, 33, 86-88

St. Peter's, Church of 5, 86, 87
Sallust, Palace of 21
Salvatio civium 24, 54-57
Sarapis, temple of 62-65
Scipio, arch of 32-33, 85-86
Septizonium 29, 74
Solomon, statue of 26, 61
Spinario 4, 23, 53-54
Sulla 31, 83

Thomas à Becket 13
Thomas de Blandeville 14, 15
Tiberius, palace of 29, 72
Trajan, Column of 7

Venus, statue of 6, 26, 59
Virgil 34, 35, 56, 64, 79, 94, 95
William of Malmesbury 39

Master Gregorius

The Marvels of Rome

Translated by John Osborne

Master Gregorius' account of the marvels to be seen in the city of Rome is one of the more interesting examples of a *genre* of literature which enjoyed considerable popularity in the late Middle Ages. An Englishman, well-versed in classical history and mythology, he recalls his own experiences visiting and examining ancient buildings and statues which still stood in Rome in the early thirteenth century. In doing so he presents a vivid picture of the wealth of classical material which still existed in the city, and frequently reveals medieval attitudes towards it.

Unlike the better-known *Mirabilia urbis Romae*, which sought to relate medieval Christian Rome to its antique heritage, Gregorius' *Narracio* demonstrates little if any interest in the city's Christian character. Instead he considers ancient art and architecture as worthy of interest and study in its own right, in many ways anticipating the antiquarian concerns of future centuries. His work is valuable both for its contribution to our knowledge of Roman art and topography, as well as in the broader context of the history of the classical tradition. The text is known from a single manuscript copy, now in the library of St. Catharine's College, Cambridge.

The translation is prefaced by a short introduction which discusses the work and sets it in its medieval context, and is followed by an extensive commentary which attempts to identify the objects and buildings seen and described by Gregorius.

Pontifical Institute of Mediaeval Studies
59 Queen's Park Crescent East
Toronto, Ontario, Canada M5S 2C4

ISBN 0-88844-281-5